A LITTLE BIT

OF

PENDULUMS

A LITTLE BIT
OF
PENDULUMS

AN INTRODUCTION TO
PENDULUM DIVINATION

DANI BRYANT

STERLING ETHOS
New York

STERLING ETHOS
New York

An Imprint of Sterling Publishing Co., Inc.
122 Fifth Avenue
New York, NY 10011

ISBN 978-1-4549-3388-5

Distributed in Canada by Sterling Publishing Co., Inc.
c/o Canadian Manda Group, 664 Annette Street
Toronto, Ontario M6S 2C8, Canada
Distributed in the United Kingdom by GMC Distribution Services
Castle Place, 166 High Street, Lewes, East Sussex BN7 1XU, England
Distributed in Australia by NewSouth Books
University of South Wales, Sydney, NSW 2052, Australia

For information about custom editions, special sales, and premium and corporate purchases,
please contact Sterling Special Sales at 800-805-5489 or specialsales@sterlingpublishing.com.

Manufactured in the United States of America

2 4 6 8 10 9 7 5 3

sterlingpublishing.com

Interior design by Gina Bonanno
Cover design by Elizabeth Mihaltse Lindy

Image Credits
Shutterstock (cover, throughout): artellia; Elchin Jafarli; Le_Mon;
Patrizia Magni; Melica; Danilo Sanino; satit_srihin; Zvereva Yana

CONTENTS

INTRODUCTION
DISCOVERING PENDULUMS

The pendulum has been used as a tool for divination and dowsing for thousands of years. The use of dowsing tools, such as the pendulum and dowsing rods, has been recorded as far back as 8,000 years. Modern use is based on the 1949 discovery by French explorers of murals drawn onto the walls of the Tassilli Caves in Algeria of people holding forked implements who appear to be searching for underground resources. The Cairo Museum holds ceramic pendulums that were recovered from tombs dating 1,000 years ago. An etching of the Chinese emperor Yu dated 2,500 years ago depicts him with a prong-like apparatus resembling a dowsing rod.

In Greece, researchers uncovered evidence dated as early as 400 BCE of pendulum use by the Pythian Oracle of Delphi, where the pendulum was used as a divination tool for royalty, nobility, and military. In the late 1500s, Italian scientist Galileo Galilei watched a chandelier swing from the ceiling of the Cathedral of Pisa, which led him study how pendulums work in the form of measuring time. His studies led to the beginning of scientific research on properties of the pendulum in the early 1600s. In the mid-1600s, mathematician Christiaan Huygens used these investigations to invent the first pendulum clock.

The pendulum, as a tool for divination, has had its fair share of critics, dating from the Middle Ages, when in early 1300 CE, Pope John XXII began persecuting "witches," people who were mainly midwives, healers, and fortune-tellers, as well as dowsers. The Church saw pendulum use as a form of divination and devil worship. Pendulum use was then forbidden until the mid-1700s CE when it became clear that pendulums were widely used successfully as dowsing rods for dowsing.

In 1833, Michel Eugène Chevreul researched the movement of the pendulum and concluded that involuntary and subconscious muscular reactions are responsible for the movement of the pendulum—making his discovery one of the earliest definitions of the ideomotor reflex. Chevreul was the first to research the pendulum in a spiritual aspect.

Abbé Alexis Mermet, who resided in France during the 1930s, had a huge success rate with the use of the pendulum in healing sessions, in helping to find missing people, and as a tool for map dowsing to find water. His work opened widespread interest in pendulums again. Now they are accepted and freely used—even by the Vatican. In 1935, Mermet was recognized by the Vatican for his extensive work with the pendulum and was asked to help solve some archeological problems! Abbé Mermet invented the Mermet pendulum— a rounded pendulum made from metal with a chamber for holding substances. The vibrations of the Mermet pendulum are thought to emit the same vibrations as the substance stored in the chamber.

Still, however successful the pendulum has been for centuries, its use is often criticized due to the lack of scientific evidence about how it works. Proving how a pendulum works can be difficult is because of the "ideomotor response"—muscle contractions caused by the subconscious movement of a person's hand.

It is very hard for scientists to gather data on this phenomenon because we cannot monitor and see energy in the form of spirit. In other words, people are unaware that they have the answers inside themselves because the conscious self likes to take over and close off the higher self and intuition. It's so easy to live this way in this day and age—our lives are so busy, and the fearful voices inside our heads can take over so easily as we get caught up in the mundane aspects of life. We forget to stop, breathe, relax, and look within when we need answers. That's why the pendulum is such a great tool, because it makes us do just that: stop, breathe, relax, and go within.

Not only is the pendulum a wonderful way to gain guidance and get answers, but it can also help locate resources. Dowsing with a pendulum is the divinatory way of locating underground resources such as water, oil, metals, crystals, and so on. This practice has been used for thousands of years. During the Vietnam War the pendulum was used to find the location of underground mines and tunnels. In France, doctors used pendulums to detect illness inside the body, a process French priest Alex Bouly termed radiesthesia in the 1930s. During the Cold War in the 1960s, Verne Cameron was denied a US passport when he wanted to travel to South Africa to help their government locate precious resources. Because he had demonstrated to the US Navy only a few years earlier how to locate every American submarine on a map using his pendulum skills, Cameron was seen by the U.S government as a national security risk. Today, the pendulum isn't used often for dowsing. Technology has become so amazing at finding resources that pendulums and dowsing rods are no longer common.

Early hypnotists also used the pendulum to relax clients into a deep state of meditation by having them watch the pendulum swing back and forth. You may have seen TV shows in which a hypnotist swings a pocket watch back and forth to bring a client into a trance. Watching the pendulum move back and forth helps to bring people into a state of relaxation by lowering brain wave activity as they focus on the pendulum, decreasing the constant mental chatter that goes on in everyday life. If you find relaxing difficult, then grab your pendulum and just watch it move. In no time, you'll be drifting off to sleep!

For divination purposes, pendulums are used to answer basic yes/no/maybe questions. Spiritually, you can contact your guides, angels, or ancestors, or whomever you resonate with in the spirit realm. Pendulums are also used in energy healing work in different modalities to balance chakras/energy points within the body and even to locate infections, ailments, and allergies. Other uses for pendulums include energy clearing of spaces, finding missing items, fortune-telling, and—some say—talking to pets! An old wives' tale is that by hanging a wedding ring or another piece of jewelry belonging to a pregnant woman on a string and dangling it over her belly, it's possible to divine the gender of her baby. This practice is still used today.

Pendulums are now gaining popularity because of their use in divination. The use of the pendulum is now widely accepted across many cultures and belief systems. The pendulum itself is not a religious tool—it's something that anyone with any belief can use.

Unfortunately, many people try to use the pendulum briefly and then put it aside, never to try again. That's because the swing of the pendulum can be difficult to interpret, and answers to questions can be indirect, particularly for those who don't yet understand the finer nuances of its function. While pendulums are very simple to use, in order to really gain the best results, you need practice, patience, belief, and acceptance that your higher self is working with you at all times to give you your answers. The pendulum is a tool to respect, to nurture, to connect with. Its simple appearance may be misleading, but you need to be in alignment with your truest form at all times— your soul and spirit. If you even for a second doubt the workings of the pendulum, then put it down and try again another time.

Pendulums are typically made in a cone shape, from metal or crystal and hung from a chain. You can use anything to make a pendulum as long as there is something at the end of a chain or string that is heavy enough to create a swinging motion. In almost every New Age shop, online or otherwise, you will find a variety of pendulums. The various forms of pendulums will be discussed later, but the first rule when finding your very own pendulum is this: listen to your heart and buy (or make) one that shines out and you connect with. You need to resonate with your pendulum; otherwise, you will be disappointed in the results. It's like anything else in life: you need to form a connection to what you are interacting with; otherwise, the energy between the two of you will not work.

So, the pendulum is a wonderful tool and one to really put your time and effort into. Like most things, it needs practice, perseverance, and understanding. This guide will help you get the most out of your pendulum, so let's delve into the world of pendulums and seek the answers that are within!

❖ 1 ❖

HOW DO PENDULUMS WORK?

A PENDULUM COMBINES A SIMPLE APPEARANCE with a mystical and nuanced function.

By responding to your body's own energetic field in conjunction with your higher self and intuition, it provokes jerk reflexes in your arm and wrist that allow the pendulum to move in a certain direction to answer your questions.

This movement in your wrists and arms is called the "ideomotor reflex," which means that the muscles in your arms are moved by subconscious activity in your brain. So by asking your question, your energy field is responding to what your inner self already knows subconsciously, but consciously you are unaware because you are so conditioned to closing off intuition and instead listening to your rational mind. Scientists have studied the concept that the pendulum swings because of the electromagnetic field on earth, much like the way the pendulum works in a clock. This is just as valid as the belief that your higher self is provoking a reaction from your brain to move your muscles; however, the latter method has not been proven scientifically yet. Both theories are based on vibrations of our energy field: the pendulum is a transmitter of energy and moves accordingly. The pendulum receives information from your auric/energy field via your higher self and beyond and then acts as a transmitter of that energy through your arm and the swinging motion of the pendulum string. Of course, the idea that the pendulum swings as an extension of spirit has its fair share of skeptics, but the more trust and belief you have in the art of using the pendulum as divination, the stronger your answers will be—so stick with it and believe that the answers always are within you.

There are too many cases to mention that support and prove that the pendulum works However, accurately measuring exactly how the pendulum works is very difficult. Testing the pendulum in a science-based environment makes it very difficult for anyone—regardless of experience using the pendulum—to make it move during the experiment, especially if attempting anything related to divination. To force the "proof" of a divination tool is extremely difficult—your body reacts negatively when it has been made to do something in a more-than-likely skeptical environment. If you are divining the future purely to prove that your system "works," the environment will become stale, and the energies of the observers have a tendency to leech into yours and corrupt your results, especially when the observers don't believe that the pendulum can work. Plus, being tested isn't exactly the most relaxing experience.

There are many factors involved in using the pendulum and understanding its movements. As mentioned before, the pendulum swings via the small muscle movements in your arm—but if you're stressed, anxious, nervous, angry, or experiencing any other emotional turmoil, these muscle movements won't work properly. To get the answers your inner self wants you to have, your muscles need to be relaxed—not fighting the adrenaline and elevated hormones in your body. The disruptions that occur in your body due to your emotions can block the energy that is used to move your pendulum, so that is why it is extremely important to stay relaxed and be in a state of emotional balance when using the pendulum. Other factors that can prompt misleading answers could be dehydration and diet. If your muscles don't have an adequate supply of nutrition and fluids, they won't move properly. Think about when you're dehydrated—your body is slower to respond, your movements are jerky, you feel lethargic, and simply put, you just have no energy. When your body doesn't have adequate nutrients to move properly, it is harder for the small movements communicated by your higher self and intuition to move the pendulum.

Another thing to consider is the placement of your arm—if your arm is too close to the side of your body, it may pick up the movements of your chest as you breathe, which can then lead to false movements in your arm. So, as you can see, it's not simply a case of picking up your pendulum and allowing it to swing. There are indeed many factors to take into consideration when learning to use your pendulum properly.

WHO HAS THE ANSWERS?

Your higher self—or intuition—works from your heart, not your head, and only brings loving guidance. Your higher self works with your guides, angels, the divine, or whomever you resonate with and knows everything about you—just like having your own personal encyclopedia, which is also known as the Akashic records. These Akashic records have everything stored about you—your past lives, your present life, and your future. As spirit guides have their own identities and personalities—much like angels, gods, goddesses, and other deities—your higher self is part of you in your etheric body (the energy layers surrounding you), which is a layer of your aura and, therefore, a part of you. Your higher self brings out the intuitive gifts inside of you. Everyone has psychic abilities, but they only manifest if you tune in and use them. Have you ever had déjà vu? Or have you ever had a gut feeling not to do something? Do you often get a strange feeling as soon as you walk into a room? This is your intuition and higher self speaking to you and giving you guidance. For some it comes easily and naturally, but for others, really trusting and listening to their abilities can take some time.

Let's take a closer look at how you can listen to your intuition. Tuning into your "clair's" (see the following list) is a great way to take advantage of the body's way of giving you guidance and pointing you toward your own psychic abilities:

CLAIRVOYANCE

Clear Seeing: Clairvoyance is the ability to see visions via your third eye (mind's eye) to perceive future events and gain knowledge about people or things. You may find it easy to visualize while you meditate, or images may just pop into your mind while you are going about your day. These images and visions are your psychic ability and the way your guides communicate with you.

CLAIRAUDIENCE

Clear Hearing: Clairaudience is the ability to hear words. You may gather and gain knowledge about future events, people, and general everyday doings by hearing words and sentences that are communicated by your guides. If you find that journaling and writing comes naturally to you, then your strongest psychic ability may be clairaudience. You may find that words, sentences, song lyrics, and poems just pop into your head easily.

CLAIRSENTIENCE

Clear Feeling: Clairsentient people have the ability to feel sensations and the change in energy in people, spaces, and the environment around them. They often feel the energies of people and spaces easily and instinctively know the mood people are in, the vibe of a space they enter, and whether something feels right or wrong, just by having a "gut" feeling about something, for example. If you are primarily clairsentient, you may feel like your own energy is being depleted constantly, especially in crowded spaces, and you need to recharge regularly.

CLAIRCONGNIZANCE

Clear Knowing: Claircognizance is the ability to just know something without having any previous knowledge about the situation, person, place, or event. Have you ever just known something about another person you've never met or a place you've never been before? People who have a strong claircognizance have this ability to just know facts as if out of the blue, can describe an event before it occurs, and simply just know when something is about to happen.

When I use the pendulum, especially for a client, my clairaudience is heightened, and I will hear words related to the client's questions. So not only do I get a yes/no/maybe answer, but also I can usually elaborate and give a more rounded and informative response based on the words that I hear. By using the pendulum for quick answers, you could actually be opening up to a whole lot more than you bargained for in a wonderful and connective way. You may be able to find your own special psychic gift as it opens up for you. Perhaps when using the pendulum you may see visions that you have never seen before, or you may have unprompted feelings in your body, or start to gain knowledge out of the blue. Be open, receptive, and trusting, and you will find that miracles can happen; life will actually begin to flow more easily and become more beautiful.

The spirit realm (as in spirit guides, angels, ancestors, gods/goddess, deities) is not moving the pendulum for you. Instead, the spirit realm is working within your energy field and your higher self to cause the tiny movements made in your wrists and arms, which is why this method of divination is so real and beautiful: you are working with it whether you think you are or not. The pendulum is not a form of magic; it is not a tool that will magically move on its own. You are moving the pendulum; it's just that you aren't aware that you are unless you are forcing the movement.

Giving yourself to this process helps bring out the spiritual aspect of your life; and over time, it can open you up to a greater scale of living. You will start to see things in a different light. When you are guided by love, you emit more love. Your connection to your higher self and spiritual guides is a lifelong relationship. Your guides are grateful that you are reaching out to them; and using the pendulum is a great tool for the kind of connection that will allow you to receive their loving guidance. Just like meditation, using tarot cards, and other methods of enhancing your psychic abilities, pendulum work can be intensely valuable. You just need to stick with it, persevere, and have belief for it to work!

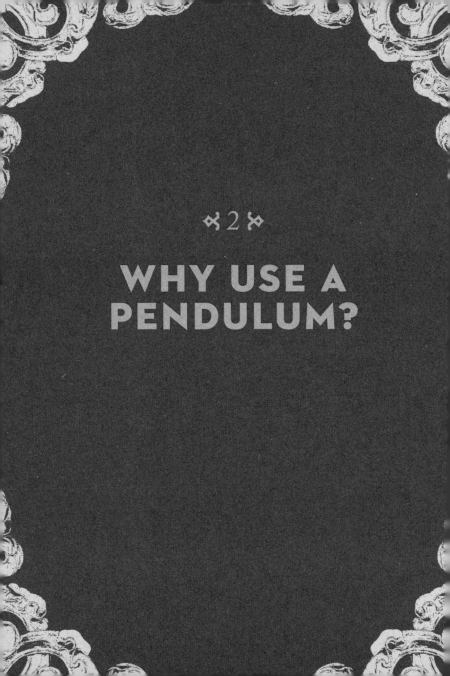

⚔ 2 ⚔

WHY USE A PENDULUM?

PENDULUMS ARE SIMPLE TO OPERATE AND ANYONE can use them. They are beautiful and mystical, and they draw people in who are curious how they work. You don't need any special qualifications to use a pendulum, and people from all walks of life can pick up the practice. Pendulums are small, compact, and affordable and can be used anywhere. While you can use a pendulum as a reliable source of guidance and information without any training, certain techniques can enhance their use and will be discussed later in more detail in chapter 5. Pendulums can be used not only for yourself in divination but also for others (with their permission). Pendulums can be used for your pets and your garden, testing food and water, and in addition to other divination tools. Let's take a look now into some different ways that you can use your pendulum:

BASIC EVERYDAY QUESTIONS

You can use your pendulum for answering basic yes/no/maybe questions such as, "Did I leave my glasses in the car?" "Should I have pasta for dinner?" "Should I buy those black boots?" Practically anything can be asked! Don't be afraid to use the pendulum for these simple questions, as this is a great way to connect and form a strong bond with your higher self and to better see how your pendulum works for you. Practicing with simple questions actually helps you gain confidence, trust, and patience with the pendulum, allowing you to grow and branch out into divination for yourself and others.

MEDITATIVE STATE

Do you remember watching movies or television shows when a magician swung his pocket watch in front of someone's face to hypnotize the person? There is some truth in this, as you can use your pendulum to get yourself into a state of meditation. The swinging motion of the pendulum helps you focus your attention and brings your mind to a state of relaxation. It helps to remove the cumbersome everyday thoughts that are constantly crowding your head. Some people find it difficult to simply sit cross-legged on a floor and focus on breathing as a form of meditation. The pendulum can be an easier alternative. Meditation takes a lot of practice, especially in this day and age, as our lives are ridiculously busy and so are our minds. It's hard for our brains to stop and be calm. Having a tool such as the pendulum to help us focus, relax, and to stop stressful thinking is a great way to start a meditation.

To use your pendulum for meditation, start by holding it in front of you and allowing it to move freely. It may move side to side or in a circular pattern. Focusing on this is a wonderful and relaxing way to get into a theta state of brain wave activity. This is the calmest state for brain waves. Throughout the day, your brain waves are usually in the normal beta state or the increased alpha state if you are anxious or stressed. By meditating, you can slow your brain waves down below the beta state and into the blissful theta state. Being in a theta state allows your brain to quiet the mundane, everyday thoughts that run through your head. This state instead creates calmness and peace and clears space for you to connect easily with your spirit guides and relieve anxiety, stress, and chaos from your life. It is important to allow your body to come into this meditative space—to wind down and actually relax your muscles, organs, emotions, nervous system, and hormonal system.

DIVINATION TOOL

Divination is the art of seeking knowledge of what the future holds, along with asking for guidance from higher sources. Divination can be achieved by using the pendulum just as it can by using oracle/tarot cards, runes, mediumship, scrying, tea-leaf reading, and so on. I find that it's easier to offer guidance with the pendulum for other people, as I tend not to have a biased view on the outcome. If you ask a very important personal question close to your heart such as, "Will I become pregnant this year?" you may be hoping for a certain answer.

If you have only just started out using the pendulum, you are more likely to move the answer to what you desire because you are emotionally invested in what you want the answer to be. Trusting that you are using the pendulum correctly takes time. You should start out asking very simple questions as mentioned before and become accustomed to how the pendulum works for you. Practicing trust with the pendulum actually means practicing trust within yourself —to allow yourself to stay focused, relaxed, and open minded. Trust me, your higher self knows when you are not in the right frame of mind to use the pendulum because—as in my case—it doesn't move at all or it literally swings all over the place!

Remember that using the pendulum for predicting the future is just like using any other divination tool—the answers you receive now may not always be the true outcome in the future. Your life always moves with your free will, and the answers that you get will be relevant for only the here and now. Your spirit guides know the best outcome for you and the best path for you to follow. It is okay to have different thoughts from the ones your spirit guides have—you are human after all. Spirit guides are here to guide you in the right direction, but you are living a life in the here and now, surrounded by many influences, distractions, and expectations. Staying on your life path and being true to yourself, not to other people, can be tough. If you stay true to your heart and yourself, then guidance with your pendulum will be easy.

WITH OTHER DIVINATION TOOLS

I love to use my pendulum with my oracle cards, tarot cards, and runes. Every day, I pull some cards as daily guidance for myself. What I like to do is get my pendulum and place my decks in a circle, making sure there is an odd number of decks so that I can tell what deck the pendulum swings to (the pendulum circle diagrams in chapter 6 give good examples of this). Another method I use is grabbing a few decks and asking my pendulum yes or no while hovering over each deck. The pendulum will then help me choose the right deck for the guidance I need for that day. Sometimes I get overwhelmed with the choice of decks (I love to buy decks of all sorts!), and sometimes I just trust my pendulum to choose for me.

I also ask the pendulum questions such as, "Should I pull two cards today?" "Is this the right question for me at this time?" "Am I interpreting the card guidance correctly?" The list goes on. The best thing about using a pendulum with other oracle tools is that there are endless ways to get guidance. Not everyone is the same, so having an individual method that suits you is the best way to work with your intuition, higher self, and guides. There is no one right way on your spiritual journey; experiment, explore, and enjoy.

ENERGETIC HEALING MODALITIES

Chakra Balance: I use the pendulum as part of my Reiki and chakra-balance sessions to assess each chakra before I work with my clients. Chakras are spinning disks or orbs of life-force energy that are based in your auric field. There are many hundreds of chakras in your energy field, but there are seven main chakras that align in the center of your body where the meridians cross. These seven chakras are associated with certain body parts, emotions, physical ailments, life situations, mental thoughts, and spiritual development. If any one of these chakras is blocked, it can cause significant disruption and disturbance in one's life. These chakra disks all have different colors and vibrate at different speeds, making them each unique. Each chakra has a matching allocated color and corresponding crystals. When placed over a chakra, about one to two inches above the body, the pendulum will spin in a circular clockwise motion if the chakra is balanced. If the chakra is unbalanced or blocked, the pendulum will spin in an irregular sideways pattern or will not spin at all.

If you find an unbalanced chakra, spin your pendulum over it three times in a clockwise direction, then counterclockwise three times, and then again clockwise three times. This shifts and disturbs the stagnant energy so that the chakra can spin freely again, allowing ease back into one's life. Once you have shifted the energy around the chakra, place the pendulum above the chakra again, and watch if it's spinning freely in a clockwise circular motion. If it is not, repeat the process until it is. Once the chakra is balanced, place the appropriate crystal over the area to boost the healing process. I do this before a Reiki session, as I feel it's an added boost of healing—the crystals work their magic while I give the client Reiki.

Reiki: Reiki is a type of healing that uses the life-force energy that the practitioner is "attuned" to via a series of symbols by a Reiki master. During a Reiki session, the practitioner emits this life-force energy via the crown of tßhe head (the crown chakra) and through the hands to the client. It's noninvasive and very relaxing and aids in the physical, emotional, spiritual, and mental healing process of the client. I use the pendulum in chakra-balance sessions and to assess what part of a client's body needs more mental, emotional, or spiritual healing, which isn't as readily apparent as physical ailments. I like to start from the crown of the client's head and slowly move the pendulum around the body to see where I need to pay more attention. As with the chakras, the physical areas in the body have links to emotions, life events, past-life situations, spiritual development, and so on. These physical areas can help pinpoint what needs to be dealt with in life. When you hover the pendulum over a client's body, watch where it spins or starts moving, as this may be an indication of what needs healing for the client. You can always do this on yourself as well.

Usually with these sessions involving the pendulum, I can focus Reiki energy on a particular area and receive messages from my spirit guides or the client's guides to help with the client's healing process. Most of the time, something as simple as a name or word can help immensely in the healing. Sometimes clients may burst out crying, and all of a sudden a stream of thoughts and ideas come into their heads that may not have ever occurred to them before. These breakthroughs release negative energy, which promptly disperses, and clients are on the road to healing a particular situation in their lives.

One of my clients felt low, like she just needed time out from being a mom. I hovered the pendulum over her body very slowly and as we got to her shoulders, the pendulum began spinning in a counterclockwise direction, which indicated blockage. While I focused Reiki energy on her shoulders, I felt an immense weight on my own shoulders, so I was feeling what she was feeling. The weight started to subside after a few minutes of energy healing, and eventually, it was gone. I received worded guidance from my spirit guides while at the client's shoulders about her sister and family circumstances; and when I then relayed the messages after her session, she just cried! She was releasing what she had been harboring inside for so long she wasn't even consciously aware she had been holding onto it. She started opening up and just let the words flow out until her face glowed. She realized what the weight on her shoulders was actually about, and once she did, she felt so much lighter and happier; she was able to focus on changing and dealing with her life more authentically.

I don't always use the pendulum with my Reiki clients, as this process can take some time. I let my intuition inform me with each client, and if I have a feeling that I need the help of my pendulum, then I will use it.

The clients are the true healers of themselves. We, as practitioners of Reiki or of any energy healing modality, are only helping to facilitate the healing. Remember, the use of pendulums or any form of oracle is only intended for guidance about healing, and it should never be used to override the advice of medical professionals or in place of it.

CONNECT WITH YOUR SPIRIT GUIDES

If you find it difficult to contact your guides, angels, or whomever you resonate with spiritually through meditation, then perhaps use your pendulum to get to know them! Ask them yes/no questions such as, "Are there more than two of you?" "Are there more than five of you?" You can then narrow down your questions as you go so you get more of a structured answer. If you do contact your spirit guides through meditation but you would like a more specific answer to the visions that you may receive, then ask away and narrow down with the pendulum.

An example would be that I had a vision of kitchens in one of my meditation sessions and couldn't figure out why I was seeing them, as I don't exactly like cooking and would rather be doing a million other things. So I asked my pendulum if I was meant to spend more time in the kitchen. And the pendulum said yes! So I asked if it was because I need to focus more on my diet. And the pendulum answered another yes. So I then asked if I should be focusing on healing my digestive system through cooking better food, and again the answer was yes. I know it sounds like a simple example, but we tend to override what is important for our bodies because we are all so busy with everything else. We tend to not actually listen to our bodies even if they're screaming signals at us. In my case, my signals were stomach cramps. This is a good example of how working with the pendulum within your meditation sessions can be so valuable.

You could also make a circle with the letters of the alphabet (one is in the pendulum circles chapter). You could ask your guides/higher self a question and allow the pendulum to spell out the answer by swinging itself to the letters. This takes time, patience, and practice, but it is a good way to communicate exactly what the answer may be. This is not a Ouija board and will not bring in bad or negative entities, so don't be fearful about using it.

Energy Clearing

There are many methods for clearing negative, stagnant, and unwanted energy from spaces and people, and using a pendulum is one of them. I like to regularly clear the negative energy in my home, such as energy from entities that are still present in this realm, negativity, and so on. Perhaps bad energy remains after an argument with a loved one or stagnant and unwanted energy from other people who may have visited or who may be surrounding the property, such as neighbors.

Sit comfortably in an area of your home (I like to sit in the middle of my home) and hold the pendulum out in front of you. Ask the pendulum to please remove any negative, stagnant, and unwanted energy from the home and for this energy to be moved to deep underground for transmutation. The negative energy will change in the earth and turn into positive energy—a process called perpetual transmutation in which energy is always in motion and changing forms. I choose the earth for the energy to be transmuted as I feel the ground beneath us gives us new life; therefore, the negative energy is given new life.

The pendulum will move differently for everyone, so just feel along with the pendulum and let it spin the way it wants. For some, it will start spinning in a counterclockwise direction; for others it may spin in a forward-back motion or a side-to-side motion. It doesn't matter which way the pendulum swings; it is still clearing the energy. Mine likes to do a combination of all motions: my pendulum starts moving in a forward-back motion, then changes to a side-to-side motion, then to counterclockwise for about five minutes. You could visualize the process of white light coming from above and surrounding you while you do this clearing. As the pendulum is swinging, visualize negative energy mixing with the white light and then flowing down into the ground beneath you.

The pendulum will then start to slow down and begin moving in a different direction once it has cleared the energy. So at this point, mine will start spinning in a clockwise direction, bringing in positive energy. If yours had moved in an up-down direction then it will move in a side-to-side direction, and vice versa, once the negative and unwanted energy has been cleared. It's also really important to put your intention into the process of removing this unwanted energy from your space, as doing so heightens the positive effects and end results.

CONTACTING ANIMALS

The pendulum can be used to connect with animals. Maybe you know that something is wrong with your pet: it is not looking well; it is not eating; it is lethargic. You could either ask questions regarding your pet or another animal in question, or you could scan its body with the pendulum slowly and notice where the pendulum spins. The spinning can give you an indication of internal issues that may need to be addressed by a vet.

DIETARY GUIDANCE

Using the pendulum can be a great way to test how fresh and wholesome your food is. Have you ever bought meat labeled sustainably sourced and organic, but you really want to make sure before consuming it? Ask the pendulum! Fruits and vegetables are the same—ask the pendulum how fresh they are, if they are ladened with pesticides (even if they are labeled pesticide free), if those particular vegetables and fruits are what you need in your diet at that time, and so on. If you feel that you may have an intolerance or sensitivity to a certain food or food groups, you could ask the pendulum once you start feeling symptoms; however, always consult a medical professional before changing your diet or self-diagnosing.

Would you like to know if the water you are consuming is okay to drink—especially if you are traveling? Hover the pendulum over the glass and ask, "Is this water safe to drink?"

I like to ask the pendulum about what type of food my body needs: "Do I need more iron-rich foods?" "Do I need to incorporate more Omega 3 into my diet?" "Are my stomach cramps from eating too many rich, heavy meals?" It may sound like very basic information that we should know about our bodies, but sometimes we just need an additional guided push to sustain our bodies better.

MAP DOWSING

As mentioned before, dowsing with a pendulum has been practiced throughout history to locate natural resources. But did you know you can do the same thing to locate missing animals, keys, and so on? Perhaps you're not sure where you would like to relocate to next or you're a little stumped as to where your next vacation should be. If so, print yourself a map that suits what you need and ask the pendulum to spin or simply make some movement over your answer. Slowly hover the pendulum over the map until it starts moving for you.

The pendulum can help guide you in your daily life and beyond. Take the time to put your energy into your pendulum. The more you work with it, the stronger your bond will become and the easier the pendulum will swing. Like everything, the pendulum works best with practice.

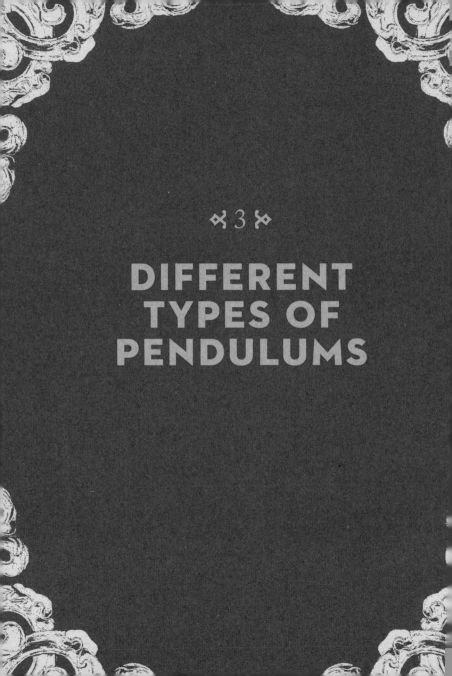

✧ 3 ✧

DIFFERENT TYPES OF PENDULUMS

THERE ARE SO MANY DIFFERENT TYPES OF PEN-
dulums out there, and it can be a little overwhelming to
choose one. There are different shapes, crystals, metals,
string options, lengths, added embellishments, and more—and all
with different meanings and added energy properties. At the end of
the day, you need to choose one that you resonate with. I have many
pendulums because at the start of my spiritual journey I was very
drawn to them. I loved the idea of using a pendulum as a divination
tool so I bought any and every one I could get, thinking the more the
merrier! This is not the case at all. I absolutely do not resonate with
some that I have, even if they are beautiful. When I use these, I just
feel a lack of connection inside of myself, and the results I get from
them are without movement or have no clear swing. Usually I will
gift them onward to someone who does resonate with them.

How do you know if you have a strong connection with a pendulum? The sense of connection is different for everybody, but in my experience it's the moment I see it and hold it. Just because you think a pendulum is beautiful doesn't mean that it's going to work with you. It's exactly like a deck of tarot cards or oracle cards—you need to resonate and have a strong feeling inside of you that the divination tool that you've chosen is going to work with you and your energy. I like to think of pendulums, and any other divination tools, as people. Everyone has their own unique energy field; and there are people we connect with and become great friends with, and there are others whom we don't connect with—our energy field and theirs just doesn't align. This is not to say that certain people, or pendulums, are horrible or have bad energy. There are simply energies that you connect with easily and energies that you don't.

Before you purchase a pendulum, it's important to hold it and really feel the pendulum's energy with yours. If you get an immediate feeling of good vibes and of a strong connection, then that's the pendulum for you. If you have found one online (which is so convenient and offers a much bigger selection to choose from), then use your intuition and go for one that immediately catches your eye. Don't overthink it. Just go with the flow of your thoughts and feelings toward that pendulum.

I have three main pendulums that I use: a clear quartz teardrop for my Reiki and chakra-balance clients, an amethyst twelve-sided pendulum that I use for divination work, and a handmade raw clear quartz-embellished pendulum that I carry around with me in my bag to use on the go. However, I also have a bowl full of them, and there are times when I simply need to use another pendulum, so I will pick one from my bowl. They are all different, but they all work on the same basic principle. Each has a unique element (usually the crystal type) that makes it great for different areas of use because of the varying energy and vibration fields of the particular pendulum.

Let's look into the different types of pendulum shapes and materials.

SHAPES

Pendulums come in different shapes and sizes, and the variety can be confusing for the beginner making the choice. Don't worry too much. There are reasons for different shapes; but any pendulum will work, as long as you resonate with it. Pendulums are nothing more than transmitters of information from your higher self; they are not the ones with the answers. Remember that when purchasing one, and don't overthink it. I like to use different shapes for each area in my practice solely because each pendulum will have a certain energy for the type of use I give it. For example, I use my clear quartz teardrop for healing as I find this shape easy to use for my clients.

You need to connect with your pendulum—so if you see a hexagonal amethyst pendulum and you immediately are drawn to it, then use it! The different shapes and sizes of pendulums are purely a guide. They can offer more to the pendulum-answering outcome,

I have noticed in my practice, but you need to use YOUR intuition always. Some pendulums are actually harder to use then others— again this is a personal experience, and I usually refer the simple teardrop pendulum for beginners, as it is easy to use. It's the perfect weight and the perfect shape to show clear answers.

Let's have a look at the different shapes of pendulums that you can buy.

Teardrop—Inverted

The teardrop pendulum is the most common pendulum that you will find in most New Age/occult shops in person and online. It is available in a variety of different crystals and gemstones and usually hangs from a silver- or gold-plated chain with a bead at the end for easy grip. The teardrop pendulum swings well because the narrow tip of the teardrop is at the bottom and the wider part is attached to the chain, therefore the teardrop is inverted, allowing for smooth motion of swing. They are also referred to as the beginner's pendulum as they are easy to use. The pendulum may also be in the shape of an actual teardrop, so the narrow tip at the top is attached to the chain and the rounded bit is at the bottom. However, these are less common and much harder to swing.

Chambered/Mermet

These pendulums are usually inverted teardrop in shape, and they have an opening at the top to put in anything that you feel will enhance your divination experience. It is also known as Mermet, as Abbe Alexis Mermet had invented this type of pendulum during his work in the 1930's.They can be made from materials such as wood, metal (silver, brass, copper), glass, or crystal.

The idea of the chambered pendulum is to enhance the divination experience by placing crystals, herbs, oils, or any item belonging to the person you are using the pendulum for, such as a piece of hair or jewelry, in it. The chamber is quite small, so whatever you are using will have to be relatively compact. By placing items into the chamber, your energy and intentions are mixed with the energy of the items you put in, and it's like a boost of pendulum power.

Here are a few ways that you can intensify your pendulum by adding items that have magical and specific energetic components to them in relation to what you want to ask. When you add these components together, you are enhancing the energies that go into making the pendulum move.

❈ Enhancing contact with the spirit world—add a pinch of mugwort, wormwood, amethyst chips, or small crystals and a few drops of frankincense essential oil.

❈ Energy clearing—add a pinch of sage, rosemary, Himalayan salt, black tourmaline chips, or small crystals and a few drops of pine or tea tree essential oil.

❈ Divining for another person—add a piece of paper with the person's name on it, clear quartz chips, or small crystals and a few drops of myrrh. Always ensure that you have the person's permission before commencing.

❈ Divining for love—add a pinch of rose petals, marjoram, jasmine, rose quartz chips, or small crystals and a few drops of ylang-ylang or rose essential oil. The best day to ask your pendulum about love is on a Friday, as this is the day magically associated with love.

❈ Meditating—add a pinch of the resin myrrh, sandalwood, frankincense, clear quartz chips, or small crystals and a few drops of peppermint essential oil.

❈ Healing/body work—add a pinch of lavender and rosemary, a small piece of bloodstone crystal, and a few drops of eucalyptus essential oil.

※ Divining for career—add a pinch of basil, cinnamon, and/or calendula, a small piece of citrine or jade, and few drops of frankincense essential oil.

Caged

Caged pendulums work in much the same way as chambered pendulums, but they are typically opened so you can see what is inside them, whereas the chambered pendulums are usually enclosed, which makes it easier to add herbs and other small items. Caged pendulums allow for the addition of larger items such as crystals or anything that you want to put inside. This shape is very popular for chakra work, as you can change the crystal in the cage to correlate with the chakra that is being balanced. For example, you can add clear quartz for the crown, amethyst for the third eye, blue lace agate for the throat, green aventurine for the heart, citrine for the solar plexus, carnelian for the sacral, and red jasper for the base chakra.

Hexagonal

These pendulums have six carved sides and an overall shape similar to a teardrop pendulum. Some people say that they look similar to a beehive. There are many different varieties of hexagonal pendulums to choose from, some made with different crystals and gemstones. The hexagon is a symbol of connection, harmony, and balance. Many use this type of pendulum for healing purposes, as it is believed that the hexagon shape can find imbalances and ailments in the body more easily. Use different types of crystals to help heal different types of ailments; for example, use rhodonite to help heal emotional scars and wounds from past lives.

Sephoroton

The sephoroton pendulum has a round sphere with a metal point at the bottom. This type of pendulum is very sensitive to vibrations due to the pointed metal tip and symmetry of the sphere on top, so it is known to be particularly accurate. The sphere shape of the crystal radiates energy from every angle, making the connection with your energy stronger, and the pointed metal tip connects with the ground beneath. Due to the sensitivity of the vibrations they receive, these pendulums are very precise and some of the most reliable and beautiful pendulums you can get.

Twelve-sided healing

These pendulums are used in the same way as the hexagonal pendulums. They have twelve carved edges and a pointed metal tip at the end. Many are engraved with different symbols such as Reiki, chakra, and other metaphysical symbols. They are used in healing and divination work. I use my amethyst twelve-sided pendulum that has a pentacle engraved on it for divination work with my spiritual guides.

Merkabah

The merkabah is a complex shape that is based on sacred geometry and said to have the shape of a three-dimensional Star of

David—two pyramids fused together to form a three-dimensional eight-pointed star. The word merkabah stems from ancient Egyptian words—mer = light, ka = spirit, and ba = body. The merkabah holds the connection to all forms of life and spirit that surround our energy field. The upward pyramid—also known as the male energy and the yang—connects us to the divine, while the downward pyramid—the female energy and the yin—connects us to the earth. This is a good pendulum to use to form higher connections to the spirit realm and for protection and healing; however, some people find this type of pendulum is harder to move.

MATERIALS

There are many different types of materials used to make pendulums, ranging from crystals to metal to wood and even to rings and keys. You can make a pendulum from anything, as long as there is a weight at the end of a string to make it swing. However, if you want to work with a pendulum and form a strong bond with it, you want it to be somewhat pretty and have a stronger force than just a key! So how do you choose which type of crystal to have at the end? Or do you use wood or metal? Just like the different shapes pendulums come in, the materials that the pendulums are made from offer different abilities in use. Pendulums are transmitters of energy into answers, so don't rush out and buy every single different pendulum on the market just because one is better for healing and one is better for divination. You must have a connection with the pendulum foremost and the rest is a bonus. So use this as a guide to determine what type of pendulum you may be after; if an amethyst teardrop is not resonating with you for divination work, don't use it!

Crystal pendulums are wonderful because each crystal has a different energy, a different vibration, and unique properties that can assist and amplify the energy the pendulum is being used for. An example would be using a rose quartz pendulum to assist in questions regarding love, romance, and friendship. It just adds a boost of energetic healing in the mental, physical, emotional, and spiritual levels of the body and mind and assists your higher self and guides.

Much the same can be said for the use of copper, brass, silver, gold, and steel pendulums. These are wonderful natural conductors of energy, and they provide a strong swing for the pendulum due to the magnetic energies of the materials to the earth's core energy and your own energetic field. These pendulums are stronger than crystal pendulums and are easier to travel with because they aren't as easily damaged.

Wood is also used and is quite popular in chamber pendulums. Wood is lightweight and is another wonderful natural energy conductor, but it does not store energy quite as well as the metals and crystals. However, it's lighter and may be a little easier for the beginner.

So let's take a look at the different materials and why they are used:

Crystals

They look beautiful and have this magical, mystical aspect to them. There are so many crystals, you can practically get a pendulum made of any kind—but here the more common ones on the market.

Amethyst

Amethyst is one of my all time favorite crystals! It's purple, it's pretty, it's easy to buy, and it's highly energetic. Amethyst is part of the quartz family and can be found in most shapes and sizes. It has the ability to clear out negative energy and bring in positive energy, which is exactly what you need for pendulum work. Amethyst is known to enhance meditation, relieve stress, enhance psychic abilities and spiritual growth, bring out that inner voice that's inside, protect from psychic attack, purify the aura, assist healings, and cleanse energy to remove feelings of fear, anger, and rage.

I love to use amethyst for my divination work. The high vibrational properties of this crystal are amazing at forming contact with a spiritual team—what I call my team "wisdom beyond." Amethyst also stimulates the third eye and crown chakras. When I use this kind of pendulum to answer divination questions for others, I almost feel the energy change when I hold it. If it feels right—use it—and this crystal feels right for me!

Amethyst is a high-vibration, spiritual-connecting stone, so the energies of this crystal at the bottom of your pendulum enhance the contact that you have with your higher self and the divine. This allows you to work with your guides to better answer your questions. It also helps you get into a meditative state more easily because of the relaxing effects and high vibrations of the stone. Simply swing the pendulum in front of your face and watch the swinging motion. Amethyst helps you overcome that busy mind of yours, get into a state of relaxation, remove negative thoughts, and allow loving and calming thoughts to come in. This crystal is wonderful to use when clearing negative energy from a room or other space because amethyst not only brings in loving energy but also repels negative energies.

Black Obsidian

Black obsidian is a wonderfully protective stone that is formed from volcanic lava. It is associated with the root chakra. Black obsidian is a superb grounding stone that enhances protection of your energy field, helps bring out that inner wisdom inside of you, and enables greater self-control. It helps you go deeper into your subconscious mind, allowing you to see the darker side of yourself and unblock and release the truth. Using this crystal as a pendulum is ideal for shadow work, which helps you see the aspect of yourself that you would normally put aside or ignore or just can't see. Ask your pendulum questions such as, "Am I feeling agitated because my significant other is being selfish?" or "Am I feeling angry because the clerk behind the counter at the store was rude to me?" There's so much scope to shadow work, but simply put: the behaviors in others (such as anger, selfishness, rudeness, annoying tendencies, over compliancy, and so on) that affect us in an irritating way mirrors our own shadow side. In general, what we find offensive in others, we are uncomfortable or unable to acknowledge in ourselves. When we delve deep within ourselves, we discover that these behaviors in others are actually reflecting our own that we simply ignore. Black obsidian can help draw out what we need to change about ourselves at a deep level.

Citrine

Citrine is the happiness and abundance stone. This yellow stone of goodness is a form of quartz associated with the solar plexus chakra. Citrine is a wonderful crystal to use for decision-making, transforming negative energy into positive energy, bringing out creativity, raising self-esteem and self-confidence, and removing emotional negativity. Citrine releases blockages and is incredibly energizing and transformational when it comes to clearing your energy field and that of other crystals as well.

Citrine is a marvelous partner to use when wanting to manifest. Manifesting is the form of visually and intentionally wanting to bring forth change into your life or having something show up that you would like to have, such as a new car, a piece of furniture, or a new friend. Use your pendulum over your vision board or any form of manifesting tool to really help create a "stir-up" of manifesting magic and power. I like to move my citrine pendulum in a clockwise direction over my manifesting visual board while I'm visualizing in my mind's eye exactly what I want. I then release my desired result like a spiral up into the divine realm for creation. Citrine enhances your concentration and mental focus (great for writers, artists, students, and teachers or to just have on your desk to gain mental clarity and focus at work). If you feel like your mind is a little scattered and all over the place, grab your citrine pendulum and use it as a meditative tool to focus your mind again. Sit and watch it swing for a few minutes, and then proceed—with a fresh mind—with what you were working on.

Great questions to ask with this pendulum would be anything to do with creating more abundance, wealth, business, success, happiness, and so forth.

CLEAR QUARTZ

Clear quartz is the most well-known crystal that you will find. This crystal can channel any type of energy; so if you're not too sure what crystal to use or if you're new to the world of crystals, look no farther than clear quartz. It is the master healer of crystals. It opens up all chakras but especially the crown, due to its high vibration. This stone amplifies the energies of all other crystals, so it works beautifully together with any other crystal to really boost energetic properties.

This is a wonderful crystal to use in healing, for clarity on things, for meditation, to cleanse spaces, to release negativity, unblock chakras, enhance psychic abilities, and receive higher guidance.

I love to use my clear quartz pendulum for my chakra healing sessions with clients, as it is the most powerful healer. This is a brilliant crystal for beginners but just as brilliant for people who are experienced as well.

Ask the clear quartz anything—there is no question you can't ask with this pendulum.

CHAKRA CRYSTALS

The chakra pendulums are made of a layering of seven different crystals—mainly different colors of agate that resonate with the seven different chakras. They are layered in the form of a pendulum weight, or the seven crystals could be embedded in the chain with a solid-color crystal as the pendulum. As the name suggests, these pendulums are used to balance and unblock the chakras. Personally, I don't resonate with these, but I have seen many other people use them. They are pretty, colorful, and come in many different formats. The idea behind these pendulums is to unblock and balance the chakras during a healing session—the chakras will resonate and vibrate to the matching crystals on the pendulum.

FLUORITE

Fluorite has many different colors, which we will look at separately. Fluorite is great at cleansing the aura and connecting you to the spirit world. It is also a wonderful healer —cleansing, purifying, balancing, and removing any negative energy from the body.

❀ **Blue Fluorite—This crystal is a beautiful calming stone that facilitates communication, creativity, and rational thought processes and it improves your connection to the spirit world. It works with the third eye and throat chakras.**

❀ **Green Fluorite—Green fluorite is a great heart-chakra healer. It opens you up to emotional healing, especially regarding love, breakups, and past hurts. It works wonderfully to clear negative energy from the aura.**

❀ **Purple Fluorite—Purple fluorite works best with the third eye and crown chakras, facilitating spiritual awakening and psychic abilities. It is a wonderful meditation crystal, so it helps you get into a relaxed state before using the pendulum for questions. It helps you focus and concentrate your mind for meditation.**

❀ **Rainbow Fluorite—Rainbow fluorite most commonly has a mix of clear, purple, and green fluorite. It's wonderful to help calm the mind; balance, rejuvenate, and cleanse the energy fields and chakras; facilitate contact with the spiritual realm and focus one's mind to the job at task. These are quite popular pendulums and easy to find in stores.**

LAPIS LAZULI

Lapis lazuli is a beautiful blue crystal with gold flecks running through it. It is associated with the third eye and throat chakra. Lapis lazuli can open the third eye, allowing the connection to spirit to be open so wisdom and guidance can flood in. It is a wonderful crystal to use to enhance communication, bring out your inner wisdom and truth, get your creative juices flowing, and enhance your psychic abilities. Use lapis lazuli to ease depression and stress—it's a wonderful crystal to create calm and peace in your life again.

Use this to help facilitate connection with your divine and higher self. Much like the amethyst, it can give your pendulum sessions an extra boost of high vibrations, making it easier for you to get into your zone of meditation and allowing you to focus and connect to receive your answers.

Lapis lazuli is also a great facilitator of seeking the truth from your mind and subconscious and for searching for real answers within. It will vibrate on the same level as your higher self, helping you get into a relaxed meditative state to receive your answers.

ROSE QUARTZ

Rose quartz is all about love—romance, friendship, family, and basically, finding love in all things in life unconditionally. As the name suggests, it is also part of the quartz family and it is a wonderful heart-chakra opener. Rose quartz is a beautiful emotional healer—great to have for letting go and forgiving, strengthening all types of love in your life, and releasing fear, guilt, and tension.

Rose quartz brings a state of deep inner healing in cases of trauma or hurtful life experiences. Place over the heart chakra, and while you do, imagine a beautiful pink light entering the chakra while the pendulum works to unblock it. You may find that there will be tears—tears of releasing and letting go. It's a great method to use when you are doing chakra work on clients, friends, family, or even yourself.

Another beautiful way to use the rose quartz pendulum is to foster harmony and love back into the life within an existing relationship. Use rose quartz if you feel the energy between you and your significant other is a little stagnant and could do with a pick-me-up. Gather a photo of the two of you, light a pink candle, and place two rose quartz pieces on either side of the photo. Spin your rose quartz pendulum clockwise over the top of the photo while you visualize harmony, love, union, and togetherness again. Once you feel intuitively that the pendulum has done its job, stop and thank it, blow out the candle, and go about your day.

Use the rose quartz to ask any questions regarding love, dating, or anything heartfelt.

SMOKY QUARTZ

Smoky quartz is part of the quartz family and really works well at both grounding and raising your vibration simultaneously. It works beautifully with the base chakra. This crystal helps ground your energy and absorb negative energy, assists in protection (especially when doing energy work), aids in meditation, helps release past traumas, and helps lift depression, stress, and anxiety. This is a wonderful pendulum to use when you need a little grounding while connecting with your spiritual wisdom and higher self. If you are very sensitive to energies around you, use smoky quartz to remove any negative energy and allow yourself to raise your vibration while still feeling grounded. Smoky quartz can also ease your mind regarding pendulum work and working with spirits.

This pendulum may be very beneficial in clearing energy around your space. A nice way to use this pendulum is to be outside (be sure the weather is not windy, as wind will make using the pendulum very difficult) in nature to get that grounding energy going through you as you sit outside.

If you have clients, friends, or family members who feel they need to be relieved of negative energy, have them lie down on their backs in a comfy position and ask that the pendulum clear the negative energy from their auras. Ask that the negative energy be transferred to the ground beneath for transmutation. Refer back to *Energy Clearing* for a reminder on how to clear negative energy.

SODALITE

Sodalite is a magnificent blue-colored crystal that works with the throat and third eye chakras. This crystal is all about opening up to all levels of communication, perceiving things better, enhancing creativity and ideas, promoting truth, and enhancing connection to the spirit realm by allowing the flow of communication to come with ease. This is especially important when working with the pendulum as you want to facilitate the transmission of the answers through you to the pendulum; so using sodalite is a great enhancer of this energy.

Sodalite is also great to use for calmness and mental ease, so use it to help ease you into meditation and relaxation before pendulum use.

As sodalite is wonderful for bringing out inner truth, it's a great pendulum to use when you're not sure of what to do—when you really need inner guidance to help you make logical decisions.

TIGER'S EYE

When I feel like I need a little (or big) boost of self-empowerment, I grab a tiger's eye pendulum. This crystal is also part of the quartz family and is associated with the solar plexus chakra. This crystal is the go-getter of crystals—it enhances personal power, courage, intuition, and "gut feelings." It helps self-confidence and self-esteem, decision-making, and aids in developing courage for new beginnings. Tiger's eye helps balance the yin-yang energy of the body and mind and also helps alleviate depression.

This is great to use when you need to add a little boost of personal power and courage to your pendulum use. If you feel apprehensive and nervous about using a pendulum, then this is a great one to employ as it gives you a sense and reassurance that the energies surrounding you and the pendulum are all safe and positive.

Metals

There are many different types of metal pendulums available, and they really have many similar properties. They are wonderful conductors and make it easier for the pendulum to move in your hand with the energy from your higher self and the electromagnetic fields that surround you. They are especially popular among map and underground dowsers. Let's take a look at the more popular metal pendulums that you can buy.

COPPER

Copper not only looks beautiful but also is a great energy conductive element. It responds quickly to vibrational shifts, allowing the swing and movement of the pendulum to be easy for anyone. Copper also has wonderful healing properties and helps to balance and clear energy. As an alternative to crystal pendulums, you could use this type in your healing and energy-clearing sessions. You will more than likely find copper pendulums in stores, as copper is relatively cheap compared to other metals.

SILVER

Silver is another brilliant energy-conducive element and has the same properties as copper. The only downside to silver is cost—silver is much more expensive than copper.

GOLD

Gold is not typically found in pendulums because of the sheer cost and because silver and copper are, in fact, more sensitive and conducive to the vibrational shifts that occur within from your higher self. But some people love gold, so if you're willing to pay a higher price for your pendulum—go for it!

STAINLESS STEEL

A lot of the spiral caged pendulums and chamber pendulums are made of stainless steel. This versatile metal is made using a mix of metals, including iron, chromium, carbon, nickel, aluminum, and silicon. It's not the pick of the bunch when it comes to choosing a metal pendulum, because it's not a single metal and, therefore, is not as energy-conducive as the others, but it still works well—especially if you put a crystal in the cage. Stainless steel pendulums tend not to build up or harbor energies like the other metals and crystals, so it can, in fact, be the best one to use in a group of people. Stainless steel is also great to use because it won't rust—and it's cheaper to buy.

So, we have looked at the different shapes and materials used for the pendulum itself and now let's look at what the pendulum is actually swinging from. Many centuries ago, human hair was used as the string to dangle the weight from, but today we have so many better options, and hair breaks very easily! You will find many pendulums are swinging from chains—silver, sterling silver, stainless steel, base metal, and so on. These are more durable and easy to see, as most pendulums these days are on a chain. If you make one yourself at home, you could use string or wool—just be sure that it is strong enough to hold the weight of the pendulum. I have made pendulums using a thin leather cord and this, too, works well. Remember that the thinner the cord, chain, or string, the better. A thick piece of chain or cord tends to decrease the movement of the weight as the energy and vibrations that help move the pendulum are absorbed more into the string than into the pendulum. Thicker string makes it hard for the weight to move at the bottom, and receiving your answers may be trickier. So look for a pendulum with a good weight at the bottom and one that it is on a thin-but-strong chain, string, or cord.

Quite a few different types of pendulums can assist your work in different ways. I do notice a slight difference with each of my pendulums based on how I want to use them, but don't be alarmed at the beginning of your pendulum journey that you don't have amethyst for spiritual work. These different types of pendulums can most certainly enhance your pendulum work, but they are not the most important factor. When in doubt, use a clear quartz pendulum if it feels right for you. Try not to use the same pendulum for all the questions, as you will more than likely find that some pendulums may not respond to certain types of questions. Find a pendulum that will work with you. For example, I will always use an amethyst pendulum for spiritual work because this is the type of pendulum that has high vibrations and loves to work with me this way.

This is purely a guide to help you choose a pendulum to work with in different ways. Enjoy the process of finding your pendulum (or two . . . or three!) Remember, the most important part is to not to overthink which one to get and to really buzz excitedly when you hold the correct one for you in your hands.

❧ 4 ❧
BEFORE YOU GET STARTED

USING A PENDULUM IS BASIC AND SIMPLE. Anyone can pick up a pendulum and let it swing between their thumb and index finger. However, I highly doubt you will get great results as there are a few factors that you have to consider before you use your pendulum. Just like any other divination tool, you need to resonate, create space, cleanse, program, and care for your pendulum. The more love and care you give your pendulum, the more your pendulum will love and care for you back. It's all about energy exchange, and if you give off negative and stale energy to your pendulum, then it will no doubt throw it back at you threefold.

Everybody has a unique and different way of using divination tools, and pendulum use is no exception to this. This is a guide to how you can create a sacred space, how to bring in your spirit team and higher self, and how to program your pendulum, but at the end of the day, you need to do what feels right for you. It's like using oracle cards—everyone shuffles them differently, some people resonate with a certain deck but others don't, some people use the same spread each day, whereas others change them daily. The same applies to the pendulum! Always remember that in order to form a wonderful relationship with your pendulum, you need to always listen to your heart and intuition. Do what feels right and don't compare your way with how others use the pendulum.

Let's get started on this amazing pendulum journey and pick the pendulum that feels right for you. Don't worry too much about the shape and material type at this point.

So you have your pendulum—now what? First, you have to cleanse the energy of your pendulum!

CLEARING AND CLEANSING ENERGY

Every living or nonliving thing harbors positive, negative, or neutral energy. Your pendulum may have been sitting in plastic wrapping in a warehouse in China for months, then been shipped via air or sea, then been transferred to either a store where you bought it or to you via mail. Your pendulum has picked up energy from quite a number of different places and people in this long process. For example, perhaps the person packaging it had a really awful set of circumstances occur and was stressed, unhappy, angry—you name it—at the time your pendulum was being packaged. That energy is now processed onto the pendulum. This pendulum is wrapped in the negativity-soaked plastic and then shipped via air or sea to its new home. The person delivering the pendulum to you might have also had a bad morning. So, this pendulum is going through a sea of emotions and negative energy from the people who are handling it. Then it arrives to you safe and sound, you open it and, in your excitement, start asking it questions—and it doesn't move or it moves all over the place!

The first thing you need to do is clear the negative energy from your pendulum. Just like clearing and cleansing your energy field regularly, the same principle applies to your divination tools. They simply will not work properly if their energy is not cleansed back to their neutral state. If I feel down, low, grumpy, and simply just not myself, I know that my energy field is clogged up with bad vibes. This happens so easily in the world we live in; and to properly function in a state of balance, we need to remove the negative and stagnant energy that surrounds us. If our sacred divination tools are clogged up with negative and stagnant energy, then trying to use them to answer your questions is like trying to take a toy away from a child—it won't work and will end in tears.

There are many ways to cleanse and clear away negative and stagnant energy from your pendulum. The following methods are wonderful to use on pretty much anything ranging from yourself to your furniture. The most important aspect while using these methods is your intention. Intention is so vital—thoughts are extremely powerful! Your thoughts create your reality. I like to set an intention pretty much before I start doing anything regarding my spiritual practice.

However, we set intentions throughout the day without really realizing it—we set the intention to call a friend, we set the intention to cook dinner and decide what to have for dinner, we set the intention to pick up the kids from school in a happy mood, and so on.

So how do you set an intention to clear away the energy from your pendulum? Start by gathering up what you are going to use for cleansing and clearing the energy (such as a smudge stick, palo santo, salt, and so on—these will be discussed more later), close your eyes, and set your intention to remove the energy from your pendulum with the help of whatever tool you are using. Ask for the energy to be removed and transferred to the ground for transmutation. You don't have to be detailed; just a few words and kind thoughts are all you need. If you set the intention in a bad mood, demanding that the energy be removed and basically being a nasty bossy boots—well, I can tell you now the energy of your pendulum will be removed but not in a great way. What you put out comes back to you threefold—a simple rule that's been around for centuries, like the age-old saying that what goes around comes around.

So, now that you have set your beautiful intention to remove the old energy from your pendulum, you now want to find the clearing tools to aid in removing negative and stagnant energy. There are a number of ways in which you can remove energy, and again, it's solely what you resonate with. So let's look at the different methods:

Smoke

Smoke from smudge sticks has been used to clear energy for thousands of years and originates with Native Americans. Smudge sticks are traditionally made using white sage, but you can also use palo santo, rosemary, mugwort, lavender, eucalyptus leaves, cedar, and sweetgrass—they all have cleansing properties. The idea behind cleansing with smoke is that the negative ions of the smoke attach themselves to the positive ions that are floating around our aura or the aura surrounding pretty much anything and neutralize them. These positive ions contribute to the imbalance of emotions, mental illness, physical ailments, and spiritual lows. So the negative ions attach onto the positive ions and neutralize them, taking away the negative and stagnant energy to another place for transmutation—usually to the earth.

You must be prepared before using your smudge stick, as you do not want embers to cause a fire in your house or the space you are cleansing (also be mindful of your hair and clothes if you are cleansing yourself!), so have a heatproof dish under your smudge stick to catch any embers that may fly out. Light the smudge stick but do not blow out the flame—allow the flame to dissipate by itself or shake it out. It should now have a beautiful waft of smoke. Hold your pendulum and wave it over the smoke until you feel intuitively that it is cleared and cleansed. Another sign that the pendulum is cleared is the movement and color of the smoke. If the smoke is thick and gray, there's quite a bit of energy to clear; but if the smoke is thin and light, there's not so much negative energy to be removed. The movement of the smoke is another sign. If the smoke has moved away from the pendulum or item being cleansed, then it's a good sign that the pendulum has finished being cleansed.

If you are in a room with a window, open the window so that the cleared energy can leave. Once you have finished clearing the energy, leave the smudge stick in the heatproof dish to burn itself out—or extinguish it in some sand or earth.

Soil

Soil is Mother Nature's gift to growing, grounding, nourishing, and clearing. We can use soil for cleansing when we send the intention for the negative and stagnant energy to be released into the earth for transmutation. This is especially potent for natural materials that are used on the pendulum, such as crystals. Place your pendulum in a beautiful part of your garden or in a potted plant if you live in an apartment, and leave it there for at least a few days. Again, use your intuition and "feel" when it's ready. Some people like to keep their treasures in the dirt for a whole moon cycle, starting with the full moon. Then they remove them and thank the earth for all that it's done. Your pendulum is now ready—maybe just dust off the dirt before use! Keep in mind if you are using this method, and it's a beautiful method—especially if you resonate well with nature, to be sure your pendulum has a stainless steel or silver chain, as you don't want any rust on your pendulum due to moisture.

Moonlight/Sunlight

This has to be one of my favorite ways to cleanse negative energy: moonlight under the full moon! It has such a beautiful, feminine, naturally soft approach to it. Full moons are the best time to release anything in your life that is not serving your higher good anymore. During a full moon, the moon is at her fullest and her most powerful. She pulls negativity away from the earth much like the way she pulls the water in the sea. A full moon ritual is a sacred way to release, remove, cleanse, and clear! Set your pendulum on the earth on the night of the full moon. A nice way to cleanse your pendulum first is to dip it in the purest water you can get. Be sure to dry it afterward as the chain or any other metal parts on some pendulums may rust if exposed to water for too long. If you live in an apartment and don't have a yard or garden, then you can either set the pendulum on a windowsill that gets moonlight or on a table. Leave the pendulum there all night and retrieve it the next morning at dawn.

Sunlight is another form of cleansing. Just think about the feeling you get when you step out into the sunlight, especially after a few days of rain and clouds, how you immediately feel rejuvenated, recharged, and happy. The same thing happens with the energy in your pendulum. This method is more rugged, harsher, and only requires a few hours of sunlight. Be careful though, as the sunlight can fade some crystals such as amethyst, citrine, rose quartz, fluorite, and smoky quartz if they are left out in the sun for an extended period. Another caution when using sunlight: some crystals, mainly the quartz family, can focus the sunlight elsewhere and spark a fire, so be careful when using this method and always keep an eye on things.

Water

Water is a beautiful way to cleanse pendulums—especially if they are a little dusty from sitting on the shelf without being used. I like to run my pendulum under the purest water I can find in between client sessions or if someone has handled and touched my pendulum. Running natural spring water over your pendulum is the most effective and purest form as the water is straight from Mother Nature herself. However, most of us aren't lucky enough to live next to a spring, stream, creek, and so on. The next best thing is to use filtered water. If you don't have access to either, then normal tap water will suffice— maybe give your water Reiki if you can or visualize white light and set the intention for the water to cleanse your pendulum. No need to submerge it under water for an extended period. While you run the water over your pendulum, always set the intention and thought process to remove any stagnant or negative energies and to restore and balance the pendulum back to its highest form of function again.

Salt

Salt is an amazing purifier and has been used for centuries to cleanse and clear away negative, stagnant, and bad energy. Have you ever seen a bowl of salt in someone's entryway? A line of salt at the entryways of people's houses? Circles of salt in a witch's casting circle or a meditation circle? This is all to remove bad energies and to stop them from coming any farther into your space. Salt is like a barrier for those nasty energies—they basically run when salt is around—as it absorbs and dissipates them. So how can we use salt to cleanse our pendulums? Grab a small bowl and pop in some Himalayan rock salt or sea salt (or any other pure salt rocks that may be available) and place the pendulum on top, or bury it underneath, and leave over night.

You can also make salty water and pour it over the pendulum as you would purified water, or take a trip to the beach and gather some seawater in a jar. While you cleanse with this water, set an intention for the saltwater to clear away any energies that do not serve the pendulum's highest good.

White Light and Visualization

Using this method is not only super fun, but it also helps you strengthen your intuitive and imaginative side, the right side of the brain. In this busy world we tend to override the right side of the brain and lose our intuition, imagination, and creativity—instead focusing only on the left, analytical and logical part of the brain. Visualization helps us to use our right side more and bring out our intuitive gifts—listening from the heart, not the head. If you're not used to visualization, then start out every day sitting somewhere quiet and imagine a white light coming from the sky and surrounding you, entering you from your aura, and making its way inside of you. You will start to feel a shift in energy; it could be tingles, temperature changes, or a sense of euphoria—whatever sensation you get will be a pleasurable one. The more you visualize this light, the easier and more quickly it will come to you, making it easier for you to visualize white light onto practically anything. You could visualize any color really; however, I like to visualize white, as it is the color of protection, purification, peace, and serenity.

Here is a quick guide to the different colors and their associations:

- ❈ White— **protection, purification, peace, and serenity**
- ❈ Yellow—**creativity, intellect, strength, energy**
- ❈ Orange—**luck, confidence, success**
- ❈ Green—**healing, balance, luck, prosperity, abundance**
- ❈ Blue—**intuition, safety, tranquility, protection, healing**
- ❈ Purple—**spiritual contact, wisdom, spiritual protection, magic**
- ❈ Red—**strength, power, passion, desire, vitality**
- ❈ Pink—**emotional support, peace, affection, compassion**
- ❈ Black—**warding off negativity, protection, binding**

I tend not to use the color black around me, only because I find it really hard to resonate with black and to visualize it. However, everyone is different and you should use a color that you feel will help remove the energies that are around you. One example is to visualize purple light around you and your pendulum if you want to remove stagnant energy and increase the effectiveness for divination and contact with the spirit world. Another could be to visualize green light around your pendulum if you use that pendulum for healing work.

The wonderful use of visualization to clear negative energy is that you have no rules to how you do it—just be sure that your intentions are always for the highest good and that you want to remove negative energy. Thoughts are just as powerful as visions!

To clear energy using visualization, sit somewhere comfy and quiet, away from distractions. Take three deep breaths in and out and ask for white light to surround you. You can either say this out loud or in your mind—both ways work well. Visualize the light beaming down from the sky and surrounding you, stopping at the ground. Visualize this light growing bigger and forming a larger circle around you. Now, visualize the light coming in from your crown chakra and filling your entire body, starting from your head and slowly working its way down to your feet, filling every cell with white light. I like to ask my wisdom beyond to join in protecting me, cleansing me, and connecting me to the divine while bathing in this white light. Now, I will focus this light to my hands as I hold onto the pendulum. I like to hold the pendulum in my left hand (receiving) and focus the white light coming out of my right hand (giving) onto the pendulum. As I am visualizing this process, I also ask that the negative energy fall away into the earth for transmutation. Once I feel intuitively that the energy has cleared and that the pendulum is back in state of balance, I thank the white light and my guides and either proceed to use the pendulum or pop it away for use another time.

Once you start getting the hang of visualizing the light to cleanse, this process can take you just a few seconds.

Sound

Using sound tools, such singing bowls, crystal bowls, Tibetan tingsha cymbals, drums, chanting, singing, bells, and clapping, can all stir up energy and allow it to reach a natural balance again. The vibrations of these tools cause stagnant energy to shift and break up and allow energy to then move on. Open a window to let the energy escape or ask that the stagnant/negative energy dissipate into the ground.

I like to place the pendulum in my singing bowl and let the vibrations work their magic, or I place the pendulum on the table that I will be working from and sound the cymbals or bells three times over it.

If you feel that the room you're in needs space clearing before you use your pendulum, then use any sound tool three times in each corner of the room. The corners tend to harbor the energy that you want gone.

Crystals

There are some amazing energy-clearing crystals that you can buy to remove negative energy from your pendulum, yourself, or your space.

Let's take a quick look at some of these crystals:

❀ **Clear quartz—I like to place a piece of clear quartz in the storage bag of my pendulum. Clear quartz is a wonderful energy cleanser and helps remove negative energy from objects.**

�֍ **Black obsidian**—Yet another wonderful crystal to remove negative energy. Boost the cleansing occurring in your pendulum storage bag by adding black tourmaline to the clear quartz.

�֍ **Selenite**—The cleansing crystal. Selenite is known as a very high-vibration crystal, making it very effective at purifying, cleansing, and removing negative and stagnant energy. It allows the space, objects, or people who are around it to stay within a balanced and positive energy field. Selenite does not need to be cleansed and should not be near water; it will dissolve. A selenite rod is very effective for cleansing pendulums, as you only have to place the pendulum on top for it to gain the benefits. You could also use a selenite wand and wave it around the pendulum to clear the energy field. You can wave it around yourself too. I immediately feel the change of energy, and it feels amazing!

CREATING SACRED SPACE

Now that we have gone over how to cleanse a pendulum, let's look at how to create a space for safe pendulum use. Some people think that by using a pendulum you are evoking negative or evil spirits, much like using a Ouija board. This is not the case at all unless you ask them to join you, but I highly doubt you want to open yourself up to that!

I love to be in my own sacred area when using my pendulum as I have channeled my energy into this area and it just feels magical to me. However, not everybody has their own room for their sacred space, and you can use the pendulum anywhere. I do recommend that if you want to start using your pendulum regularly, finding a sacred space will make your pendulum feel a whole lot more special.

Let's look at how you can set up a sacred space. As mentioned before, not everybody can have a whole room dedicated to spiritual work. So I would like you to find a beautiful spot in your house or apartment—anywhere you feel intuitively pulled to create space. It could be a corner in your bedroom or a space in your lounge room—anywhere! Gather items that have a special meaning in your spiritual practice. These could be crystals, candles, figurines, special mementos, wands, shells, cauldrons, incense burners—honestly, anything that makes your heart sing! Place them on the floor, on a table, or anywhere you want, on top of a beautiful piece of fabric or lace and perhaps lay a beautiful rug and place cushions around them. This is your space and this is where you are going to channel your beautiful energy. Use your heart and gather and decorate the space to match who you are.

I use my pendulum both at my table and on the floor in front of my altar. I have found that both areas serve my pendulum work well. You may read elsewhere that you need to sit at a table with your elbow resting on it, and both feet uncrossed on the floor. This is highly recommended for beginners as a way to make your body more stable (and it's more comfortable). However, I love to sit on a cushion on the floor with legs crossed, allowing my elbow to rest by my side. Even though my legs are in a crossed position, my body feels firmly grounded; and I still feel the energy flow fluidly inside and around me. Everyone is different, so sit however you feel most comfortable. I will focus on sitting at the table.

You have your pendulum and you're at your table. If you feel that the energy in the room needs cleansing, then use one of the methods mentioned previously to shift and remove the stagnant energy. This is vital as you want your surrounding energy fields to be positive, free flowing, and negative-energy free. You don't want this energy to interfere with your pendulum work. Sit at the table and make sure your spine is straight, your feet are touching the floor and are uncrossed (this helps you feel grounded), and your elbow is perched comfortably on the table.

Before I start using my pendulum, I like to go through a quick white-light visualization and I imagine a circle of white light surrounding me for protection. I then ask my wisdom beyond to join me. You can ask whomever you resonate with or work with spiritually to join you. I love to sit for a few minutes in a breath meditation, in which I take a few deep breaths in and then out. I then focus on my breathing and the swing of my pendulum for a few moments to center myself, calm my thoughts, and focus my intentions on the pendulum. It's important to get into a state of meditation before using your pendulum as you want to limit your thoughts calm your emotions, and you want to create a space where you can focus on the pendulum 100 percent.

When I am meditating, I love to light candles and burn dried herbal incense. The magical components of the herbs can help raise my energy, as well as that of the space around me and my divination tools. Here are a few recipes that you can make up at home. Place an equal amount of herbs in a jar, mix together, cover tightly, and store for future use. If you don't have all the ingredients, just mix together what you have. Light a charcoal disk that you can buy from most new age shops and place it in a fireproof and heatproof dish or cauldron. Once the charcoal is lit, place a pinch of the dried herbs on top, adding more as needed.

Meditation Incense Blend

I love this blend to help me get into a relaxed mood and to also call in my spirit guides. Mix together in equal amounts:

❋ Frankincense   ❋ Wormwood

❋ Sandalwood   ❋ Cinnamon

❋ Mugwort   ❋ Spearmint

HEALING INCENSE BLEND

This is a beautiful blend to have burning while using your pendulum in healing sessions such as Reiki and chakra balancing. Mix together in equal amounts:

❋ Myrrh   ❋ Sage

❋ Lavender   ❋ Thyme

❋ Chamomile   ❋ Rosemary

❋ Rose petals

CLEARING ENERGY BLEND

This blend is a wonderful accompaniment when using your pendulum to clear negative and stagnant energy in your home, on yourself, or on objects. Mix together in equal amounts:

- Sage
- Rosemary
- Lavender
- Eucalyptus
- Patchouli
- Frankincense
- Myrrh
- Sandalwood

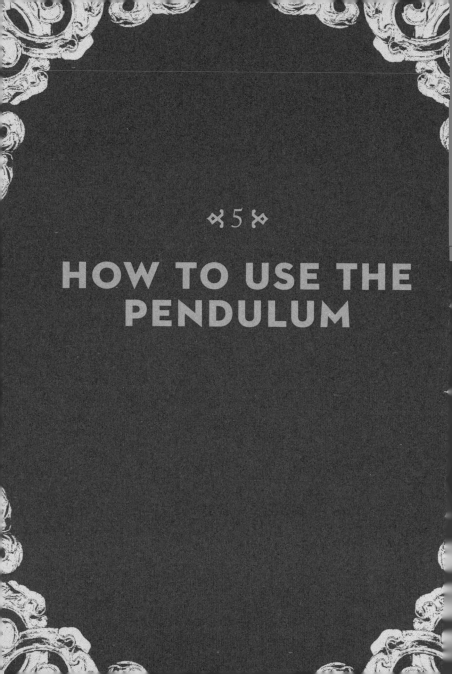

❖ 5 ❖

HOW TO USE THE PENDULUM

NOW THAT WE HAVE SET THE SCENE AND CLEARED the energy, it's time to hold your pendulum and let the magic begin.

PROGRAMMING YOUR PENDULUM

Once you feel ready, hold your pendulum at the top—there's usually a little bead, bell, or some small item for gripping. Use your thumb and index finger of your dominant hand to hold the top of the pendulum and rest your elbow on the table. Your wrist should remain straight and your elbow should be slightly bent. Your arm should look fairly straight and be aligned from your hand to your elbow. Your grip on the pendulum should be relaxed and not too tight, as you want the pendulum to freely move without constrictions.

Now that you are in a comfortable position, the next step is to program your pendulum. This simply means finding out how the pendulum swings for your yes, no, maybe, and not now answers.

I like to ask the pendulum to show me a yes, and my pendulum swings forward and backward. I then ask it to stop. Once it has, I then ask it to show me a no, and my pendulum swings left to right. I proceed to ask it to show me a maybe, and my pendulum swings in a counterclockwise direction. My pendulum doesn't move at all when I ask for a not now answer.

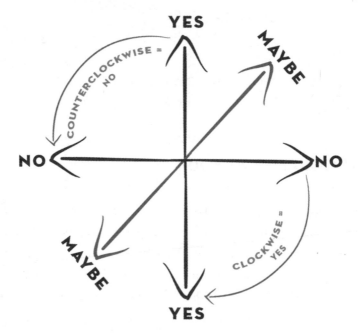

Everybody is different, so that is why each of us needs to program our pendulum before starting. A few times, especially at the beginning of my pendulum journey, the pendulum would change movements for the yes/no questions. Sometimes my pendulum would spin in a clockwise direction for yes answers and a counterclockwise direction for no. I always program my pendulum before use. The way it swings could change any day, and I might be interpreting the answers wrong!

The beauty about programming your pendulum is that you get a feel for how the pendulum moves. I've witnessed many times the disbelief and the amazement on people's faces when they use the pendulum for the first time and it starts swinging. They can't believe that the pendulum's swing is so strong when they are not forcing the movement.

GETTING TO KNOW YOUR PENDULUM

It's important the first few times using a pendulum to really get to know how it swings and to practice focus, patience, and trust. Picking up the pendulum and asking it questions straight off often won't work. It's so important to practice and slowly get familiar with the pendulum—and then it'll be easy to use when you get into the swing of it!

Give your pendulum a weeklong "getting to know you" period. Asking important questions of the pendulum requires a lot of focus, patience, and trust, all of which can be very hard when you're new to pendulum work. You want answers straightaway—so instead of easing your way into it, you go straight in and may in fact be swinging the pendulum yourself for the answer you want. On some occasions, I have witnessed people using a pendulum for the first time, and the answers they got were true for them—so you ask, "why then do I have to practice if people can actually start straightaway?"

So yes, you can start straight away; but you should really form a bond and trusting relationship with the pendulum first. It's very different from oracle- and tarot-card work as you can't see the pictures or the cards' meanings when you shuffle and pull them. The pendulum is right there, and you can see it swing. In fact, you have to focus and watch it swing! Also, everybody is different. Some find it hard to focus, while others find it very easy right away. When people ask a question with the pendulum the first time, they don't really know what to expect, so the answer will most likely be true. The more they ask, the less likely the pendulum will move for them, because they are now thinking about the swing and the answer and not relaxing into the process the way they did at the beginning.

But by gradually easing your way into the feel of your pendulum, you then start trusting yourself and letting go of expectations and urgency. You get to a place where the pendulum swings and you just let the process occur naturally.

Set aside about fifteen minutes each day the first week to sit in your sacred space and spend time with your pendulum. Not only is this going to be a wonderful experience for your pendulum journey, but also it's a wonderful way to allow you some time to slow down, meditate, and form a bond with your higher self and spiritual team.

Getting to Know Your Pendulum Exercise

Start by cleansing your environment, yourself, and your pendulum. After daily rituals of removing negative energy from yourself, you will find that your moods, your energy, and your well-being will be totally uplifted! Sit in a comfy position in your sacred space. Meditate for however long you feel and try to switch off from the day you have had. Concentrate on your breathing, and whenever thoughts enter your mind see yourself releasing them to the ground.

Once you are ready, hold your pendulum and program it. Once you have programmed the pendulum, ask it really basic questions about your day so that you get yes/no/maybe/not now answers. It's best to ask questions that you know the answers to so you get a feel for the pendulum—how long it takes to swing, how it swings, if the questions you're asking are right for the pendulum, and so on. If a question you ask is vague, like "Should I take this job or the other job I applied for?" or the question just has unclear content in it, then you will find the pendulum will not move or will move chaotically. Be sure to always word your questions with confidence, use correct grammar, and make sure that your question is closed-ended and makes sense! The pendulum swings differently for everyone: for some the pendulum will make huge swings. For others, the pendulum may only swing gently, so don't be alarmed or assume you're not doing it right if your pendulum doesn't swing madly for you. With practice and time, your pendulum will start to swing in leaps and bounds in response to your questions.

Once you feel that you are forming trust within yourself to allow the pendulum to move freely, that you are relaxed when using the pendulum, and that you are in a state of open mindedness, then you are ready to tackle any question with your pendulum.

Finding an Object Exercise

Grab a partner—it can be a friend or family member—and ask the person to hide an object somewhere in your home. Once this object is placed somewhere, sit in meditation, program your pendulum, and start asking questions about the object's location.

Some questions could be, "Is the object in the bathroom?" "Is the object in the potted plant in the bathroom?" and so on, until you feel you have reached the point of knowing where this object was placed—now go and see if it's there! Again, do not be disappointed if you don't find your object on the first try—this is an exercise and it requires practice, just like everything else. Persevere and once you get it, there's no stopping you!

A great tip when using the pendulum to ask questions is to write the questions down and then write the answers next to them. If I ask lots of questions in a session, I can actually forget what the answers were to the previous questions, so I can accidentally ask the same question twice. This wastes time and may suggest you're not trusting what your guides are telling you. The whole idea is to have trust with the answers the pendulum gives you. Write down in your journal some questions to start with and then flow from there.

Once you have finished your session with your pendulum—whether it was to answer questions, clear energies from a room, or use in healing work—always thank your higher self and guides for assisting you. It's a great practice to then start the cleansing process of your pendulum after your session by removing the energies that you and the pendulum could have picked up while working with it. Choose one of the methods mentioned in earlier in this chapter, "Clearing and cleansing energy."

WHAT TYPE OF QUESTIONS SHOULD I ASK?

The questions you ask your pendulum should be short, articulate, and to the point. Ask closed-ended questions--ones that receive yes or no answers.

Some examples:

- ❈ "Should I wear red shoes today?"
- ❈ "Are my keys in the kitchen?"
- ❈ "Is my strongest psychic ability clairvoyance?"
- ❈ "Will I receive that important email about my job today?"
- ❈ "Should I change jobs?"

These easy questions can then lead onto other closed-ended questions to give you more guidance to what you seek. More examples:

- ❈ "Should I leave my current job?"—Yes
- ❈ "Should I go back to study?"—Yes
- ❈ "Should I study teaching?"—No

❈ "Should I study counseling?"—Yes

❈ "Should I get a part time job while I study?"—Yes

And so forth until you feel happy and content with the guidance you have been given. You already know the answers to the questions being asked—the answers lie within. If you really dislike your job, it's the fear factor in your head that is stopping you from leaving it. The pendulum can give you that push of confidence to actually start listening to your heart instead.

Never ask questions in relation to other people unless you have been given permission to do so. Don't ever ask a question that may violate someone's privacy or free will. An example would be, "Is Emma's boyfriend cheating on her?" This is a recipe for disaster and not your place ethically to be in. If Emma wants you to ask the pendulum if her boyfriend is cheating on her, kindly refuse, as using the pendulum to answer this kind of question will backfire and it is not the right question for pendulum work.

Also, steer clear of open-ended questions such as

❈ "What should I do if I quit my job?"

❈ "What pet should I get?"

These questions are too confusing for your higher self to answer with the pendulum, and the answers will not be accurate. The pendulum will most likely not move because it is unable to respond.

When asking important, major life questions such as, "Will I become pregnant?" try not to put time constraints on these types of questions. Instead of asking, "Will I become pregnant in the next cycle?" ask, "Will I get pregnant at some stage?" This allows you to relax, and you won't be putting pressure on yourself or your partner. Plus, you may be setting yourself up for disappointment because you may have inadvertently moved the pendulum to see the answer you wanted. Asking important life event questions is probably best left to somebody else who doesn't know you. There are plenty of people on social media and online who offer pendulum sessions, so why not take advantage of these sessions if you don't think you can answer something yourself?

Love questions are also a very touchy subject. Do not impede somebody's free will or energy; it's like doing a love spell. Feel free to ask questions about love, but aiming your questions toward one person in particular is a not a good idea. Instead of asking, "Does Nick love me?" ask, "Will I find romantic love in the next six months?" The universe may not want you to be with Nick, even if you think he's gorgeous and you really want him to be your partner. There may be someone even better for you!

A good example of not wording your questions properly is this: You ask your pendulum, "Will I find love in the next few months?" The pendulum answers yes. Great, so you're excited now because you're going to find love with someone and live happily ever after. So a few months go by and you still haven't found love with someone. But the pendulum said yes! So you think you wasted your time and that the pendulum didn't work. But in those few months, you formed a new friendship with someone and that someone has been super important to you. Plus, you found a cat and now she is your pet and you couldn't imagine life without her. So, you have indeed found love but in a different way from what you thought!

The wording of your questions is very important in gaining more clear and precise answers from the pendulum. Be very specific with what you want to ask. For example, if you want to find romantic love with a partner, then ask, "Will I find myself a romantic partner to love in the next few months?"

Also, remember that if your pendulum doesn't answer some of your questions, it's likely because the pendulum best answers most questions in the here and now. It's like most other divination tools—you can ask questions regarding the future, but free will always plays a part in your life, and things change all the time. There are paths to follow, and a lot of the time, there are forks in the road. Your higher self and guides can help you choose the right path. You have free will and you are living in the now, so you may choose another path, in which case your guides can then only help you navigate that path the best they can.

Do remember that the pendulum is handled and operated by us—humans! We all make mistakes and pendulum use is no exception. Using the pendulum doesn't mean that you will always get the right answer—even if you're a pro. Yes, the more you use it the more accurate your answers will be. The pendulum is accurate most of the time, but you as the human operating the pendulum can sometimes misinterpret your guides or have your guides misinterpret your questions. Don't let misinterpretation affect your pendulum work. Keep at it, keep believing, and know that your pendulum is a wonderful divination tool!

TOOLS TO HELP RECEIVE ANSWERS

There are different ways to help you receive your yes/no/maybe/not now answers from your pendulum. Many different pendulum mats, boards, and circles are available in New Age shops and online that can assist your pendulum work. These tools are a great way to help the beginner and the experienced user receive clear answers with a pendulum. They are great fun to use and add a different spin to receiving answers.

Pendulum mats and boards typically have diagrams that include yes/no/maybe/not now, the alphabet, numbers, astrological signs, days of the week, and so forth. These are not Ouija boards; you are using your energy via the pendulum, not the energy from the spirit world via the glass planchette. Pendulum circles are divided into an array of an uneven number of wedges that you can fill in with different possibilities to obtain an answer. There are filled-in pendulum circles in chapter 6 that you can use and blank ones that you can create for yourself.

STORING YOUR PENDULUM

Think of your pendulum as a new best friend. Treat it with respect and with care. Your pendulum, like anything you touch, picks up your energy, so why not give it the best energy you have? Create a spot in your sacred space for it. If you're creative and good with a sewing machine, make a beautiful little drawstring bag for your pendulum—it can be velvet, cotton, linen, hemp, or whatever you love—or buy a pouch if you can't make your own. Place a clear quartz or selenite crystal in the bag for further cleansing while you're not using your pendulum. If you leave it in a place that is loud, crazy-busy, and simply buzzing with other people's energy, the pendulum may buzz right back at you when you want to use it—even if you have cleansed it after its last use. You want your pendulum to be at its optimal energy level for use so treat it with love, care, and appreciation. If you have picked a crystal pendulum, always be mindful of where you put it, as you don't want it to chip, especially at the tip.

WHAT IF MY PENDULUM DOESN'T WORK?

There will be times when your pendulum either doesn't move or spins and swings all over the place—not really making any sense to you whatsoever. So how do you stop this from happening?

❊ Try not to use the pendulum when you are tired, anxious, feeling down, or depressed, as this may hinder your answers.

❊ Do not be under the influence of alcohol or drugs

❋ If you have limited your belief about the pendulum actually working, then more often than not, your answers will not be accurate Be sure to have cleansed and cleared your energy and the pendulum's before use.

❋ Your higher self might know when you're not in the right frame of mind to use your pendulum. Even if you feel you are, your higher self always knows better.

❋ Use another pendulum. Perhaps the one you are using is not the right one for the type of questions you are asking, or it simply is not the right pendulum for you to use. Listen to your intuition always.

❋ The pendulum you are using may not be the right weight for you. Try ones with different weights and see how they feel in your hand.

❋ Adjust the length of the pendulum string/chain. Sometimes when it is too long, it doesn't swing as easily, so shorten the length of the chain and see if that helps. When the chain/string is too long, the pendulum can take longer to start swinging; and if you are only just beginning to learn the pendulum, this can be quite frustrating. The swing may be quite faint when the chain/string is too long, making it harder for you to determine your answer. You could start by twisting the chain around your finger to shorten it and then trying again. The chain/string should be about 7–8 inches long

❋ The timing may not be right. Maybe you are rushed and you only have ten minutes before you have to be somewhere, but you want a quick check with your pendulum. Don't ever rush an answer from your pendulum.

I had mentioned previously that using your pendulum when you are down or just not in the right frame of mind could hinder the results—it can actually do the opposite as well. You do not always need to be happy or vibrating high to use your pendulum! Being relaxed helps better your energy flow for the pendulum, but don't be afraid to use your tools in times of need. Often in the past when I was feeling stressed, anxious, or just not myself, I didn't seek the help of my divination tools. But over time, I have learned that these tools are in fact the right tools to help me get through my hard times, however not without a lot of practice and use beforehand.

Sit in meditation for a while, compose your thoughts again, and then ask away. When you're feeling anxious and you would like some reassuring answers from your pendulum, take a few deep breaths in and out and focus on your breath work for a few minutes. Imagine the breath going into your heart chakra. This is a great way to lower your heart rate and to help get you into a state of relaxation.

If you want more reassurance, then grab a deck of oracle or tarot cards and pull some cards along with seeking answers via the pendulum to give you more guidance. However, if your pendulum just does not move while you are feeling down, then chances are that your higher self knows you really need to work on raising your vibes before you try again.

Patience, discipline, openness, a neutral state, and focus are all vital to the use of the pendulum, regardless of what your mood is like. If you are focusing on the day's events instead of the question at hand and the answer you're about to get, the pendulum likely will not move or will swing in ways that will get your attention to focus. Pendulum use is a discipline, and it requires practice and patience. Yes, having something swinging from your fingers might sound and look easy enough, but the way you project your thoughts and get in tune with your inner self is what is going to make pendulum use easy. You want the right answers and you want to trust the pendulum to give you the right answers. If you are not dedicated to using the pendulum with all your inner might, then you might as well leave it at the store. If you have the slightest disbelief, then your inner self and higher guides also pick that up and won't come to the party. Trust, believe, be patient, learn, focus, be disciplined, relax, and most important, enjoy the relationship you have with your spirit guides via your pendulum.

✦ 6 ✦

PENDULUM
CIRCLES

PENDULUM CIRCLES ARE A GREAT WAY TO RECEIVE answers as well. They go beyond the yes/no/maybe/not now answers. You can make a circle about anything—chakras, crystals, moon cycles, spells, love, career, colors, activities—the list goes on. The circle has to be split into an uneven number of sections so that the when the pendulum swings it has one answer to give you instead of two. Divide the circle into around nine to eleven parts— that way it's easier to notice where the pendulum is swinging. I have provided a few circles for you to use and a few blanks so you can make your own. Another alternative is to draw a circle on a piece of paper and fill it in yourself. When you set the pendulum over the circle, allow the pendulum to hover at the center of the circle no more than an inch above it. The lower your pendulum, the easier it is to determine which wedge of the circle the pendulum is swinging toward.

I have noticed when I do this after asking my question, my pendulum tends to swing in a clockwise movement in the center of the circle, almost like it is trying out each answer given in each wedge. This can take up to one minute, so be patient with your pendulum. Once it has finished swinging in the center, it starts to move in different directions and then focuses movement on a particular wedge. If I am not sure exactly which wedge the pendulum is angling toward, I focus my eyes downward—like a bird's-eye view over the pendulum and onto the circle and close one eye. This way I can see more clearly where the pendulum is swinging. If that doesn't help, then I take note of the two possibilities and ask the pendulum, "Was the answer you provided for me in section #2?" and so forth.

SIMPLE YES/NO/MAYBE/NOT NOW

This circle is a great one for the beginner to start getting a feel for the pendulum's swing. You could just use this diagram or make up another like it to use at all times—your choice.

YES—The answer to your question is yes.

NO—The answer to your question is no.

MAYBE—The answer to your question is maybe. Perhaps ask another question in more detail or word the question again so that it has a clearer meaning.

NOT NOW—There could be two ways your pendulum responds not now—either it swings in the direction of Not Now or it stays stationary. Not now answers occur mainly in response to very personal questions that want a specific answer but that the pendulum may not be the right divination tool to address—so perhaps try oracle or tarot cards.

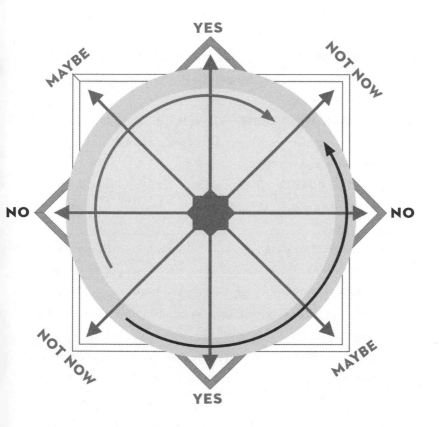

Clockwise = **YES**   Counterclockwise = **NO**

CRYSTALS

Use this circle to find out which crystal will best serve you for the day ahead.

AMETHYST—intuition, third eye, calms emotions, aids in meditation, helps ease headaches, aids detoxing, improves focus, and aids in dream work.

CITRINE—happiness, abundance, wealth, enhances self-esteem, solar plexus chakra, boosts creativity, manifestation, and aids in decision-making.

GREEN AVENTURINE—a great healer, calms emotions, heart chakra, opens one up to love, abundance, and aids in relaxation, money, luck, and success.

ROSE QUARTZ—friendship, heart chakra, aids in emotional healing, compassion, calmness, peace, romance, harmony, and nurturing.

CARNELIAN—courage, sacral chakra, boosts self-esteem and confidence, eases aggression and anger, and increases personal power.

RED JASPER—strength, base chakra, boosts survival instincts, stability, protection, grounding, and aids in astral travel and meditation.

SODALITE—balances emotions, throat chakra, communication, aids in hypersensitivity, intuition, knowledge, and meditation.

SMOKY QUARTZ—grounding, helps protect from negativity, relaxation, and aids in improving mood.

MOONSTONE—brings out your feminine energy, soothing, calming, intuition, love, release, wisdom, insight, and boosts creativity.

MOON PHASES

Use this circle to work with the moon. You could ask this circle when a good time is to cast a certain spell, to do certain types of work in the yard or garden, to release, to expand, to seek new work, and so on.

NEW MOON—This is a time for new beginnings and new growth. Start new projects and manifest what you want to bring into your life.

WAXING CRESCENT—Visualize your dreams coming true. Have courage and faith that what you want will come to fruition.

FIRST QUARTER—Take note of any difficulties that may arise in your life and have the confidence to see the greater good. Build, grow, and nourish.

WAXING GIBBOUS—This period is all about focusing on your outcome and expanding and changing as you grow. Just flow with life.

FULL MOON—Release anything that stands in your way. Power and energies are heightened.

WANING GIBBOUS—Be gentle to yourself and relax. Remove the unnecessary from your life, and just breathe.

LAST QUARTER—Harvest the goods that you have sown—relish what has been given to you and make way for the new.

WANING CRESCENT—Surrender to the powers that be and allow yourself the energy to start fresh again.

DARK MOON—(a day before the new moon) A time for self-reflection, hibernation, and renewal.

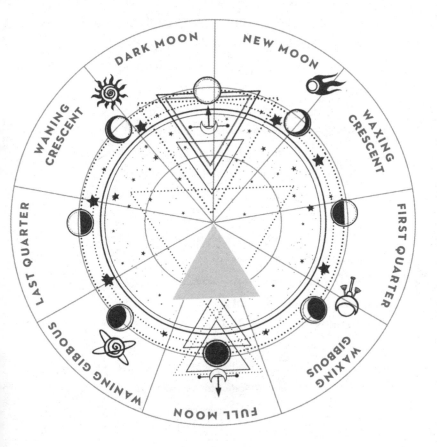

DARK MOON

NEW MOON

WANING CRESCENT

WAXING CRESCENT

LAST QUARTER

FIRST QUARTER

WANING GIBBOUS

WAXING GIBBOUS

FULL MOON

Pendulum Circles

CHAKRAS

This circle is to help you find out which chakra needs attention, balancing, or clearing or which chakra and the associated crystals, essential oils, and so on will assist your day greatly.

CROWN CHAKRA—consciousness, wisdom, enlightenment. Crystals: clear quartz, amethyst. Essential oils: frankincense, juniper, ylang-ylang. Plants: lavender, rose, lotus.

THIRD EYE CHAKRA—intuition, psychic ability, knowledge. Crystals: amethyst, lapis lazuli. Essential oils: lavender, rosemary, frankincense. Plants: mugwort, violet, eyebright.

THROAT CHAKRA—communication, creativity, truth. Crystals: sodalite, blue lace agate. Essential oils: peppermint, tea tree, thyme. Plants: sage, peppermint, clove, star anise.

HEART CHAKRA—love, relationships, compassion. Crystals: rose quartz, green aventurine. Essential oils: eucalyptus, chamomile, lime. Plants: jasmine, gardenia, rose.

SOLAR PLEXUS CHAKRA—confidence, power, courage. Crystals: citrine, yellow fluorite. Essential oil: lemon, lemongrass, chamomile. Plants: lemon balm, pennyroyal, cinnamon.

SACRAL CHAKRA—emotions, pleasure, motivation. Crystals: carnelian, orange calcite. Essential oils: geranium, coriander, rosemary. Plants: nettle, yarrow, allspice.

BASE CHAKRA—security, grounding, stability. Crystals: red jasper, smoky quartz. Essential oils: vetiver, patchouli, sage. Plants: rosemary, valerian, patchouli.

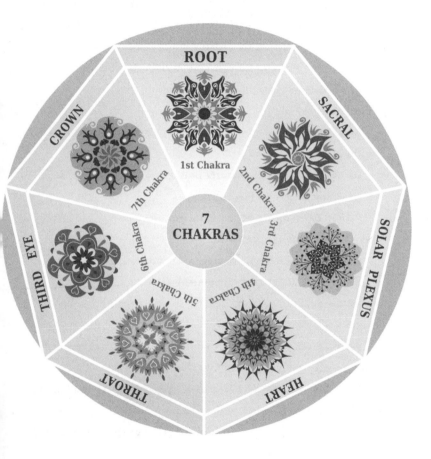

ROOT

CROWN

SACRAL

1st Chakra

7th Chakra

THIRD EYE

6th Chakra

7
CHAKRAS

2nd Chakra

3rd Chakra

SOLAR PLEXUS

5th Chakra

4th Chakra

THROAT

HEART

COLORS

We use colors every day for various reasons. Each color has unique qualities that can help us emotionally, mentally, physically, and spiritually. Perhaps you're not sure what color to wear or what color will help uplift your mood. Let the pendulum find the answer for you!

BLACK—protection, , transformation, endings, rebirth, release, strength.

BLUE—calming, knowledge, finding truth, communication, intuition, clarity.

GREEN—abundance, nature, prosperity, luck, fertility, acceptance, healing, peace, well-being, success.

PURPLE—spirituality, magic, psychic powers, divination, wisdom, truth, intelligence, authority.

ORANGE—ambition, courage, endurance, energy, power, optimism, stimulation, action, abundance.

RED—vitality, passion, assertiveness, strength, willpower, determination, sexual energy, love, lust, desire.

PINK—love, relationships, nurture, affection, emotions, compassion, peace, sympathy, harmony.

YELLOW—happiness, creativity, prosperity, concentration, inspiration, power, learning, willpower.

WHITE—purity, peace, cleansing, harmony, spirituality, birth/death, power, wholeness, unity.

BLACK BLUE GREEN PURPLE ORANGE RED PINK YELLOW WHITE

Pendulum Circles

91

CAREER

Sometimes we just need a little boost to help further ourselves on our path, and our careers are a big part of our life path. On average, we can change jobs ten to fifteen times in our working life; and I bet we dislike most of those jobs. A lot of aspects affect what we do for a living, so let's ask our higher self every now and then to give us a guiding nudge to help us onto the next step.

STAY PUT—This job serves well, so stay put for now.

BE BRAVE—Time to fly, spread those wings, and journey high, whether it be asking for a raise or a promotion or looking elsewhere.

TAKE THE RISK—Follow your intuition and see what else is out there for you. Follow your heart.

MOVE ON—This job no longer serves your higher good so perhaps now is the time to call it quits?

RAISE THAT DOLLAR—Cha-ching!!! Either a bonus or raise is coming your way or now is the time to ask for one!

IMPROVE KNOWLEDGE—Perhaps going back to college is a good idea, or attending workshops, seminars, or anything that will improve your knowledge base.

CHANGE IS ON THE WAY—Listen to your heart and go with the flow. Change is about to happen, so be open to what is offered to you.

ALLOW HELP—Now is the right time to ask for help. Don't think you need to do everything yourself; decrease the workload if need be.

LADDER RISING—Put in your application because you never know!

LOVE

Many of us need a little help in the love department, and there's no better way than to ask your spiritual guides for some loving advice.

STOP LOOKING—You have either found a wonderful soul connection with someone already or you need to stop looking for a partner, as the act of looking may actually be hindering a connection with someone.

LOVE IS COMING YOUR WAY—Breathe and relax into this situation, as love is just around the corner if you open your heart and eyes to what will be placed before you—probably in unexpected ways.

MOVE ON—You may be in a relationship at the moment that is not in your best interest, so perhaps let go of it. Someone else is out there waiting for you.

ALLOW SPACE—You may need space to reconnect with someone again. As the saying goes—absence makes the heart grow fonder.

FULL HEART—You are exactly where you need to be right now. Enjoy this loving union you have with your special person.

LOVE SPELL—Maybe its time to whip out the *Book of Shadows* and cast a spell to bring love into your life. Remember, never cast a spell that may interfere with someone else's free will!

TRUST—Trust that everything is going to be okay! You may have trust issues with your partner, and this may be a sign to trust your inner intuition. Listen to your heart.

STOP LOOKING

LOVE IS COMING YOUR WAY

MOVE ON

ALLOW SPACE

FULL HEART

LOVE SPELL

TRUST

1
2
3
4
5
6
7

MEDITATION AND RELAXATION METHODS

Meditation methods are different for everybody. Perhaps there are a few methods that you love but you're not sure which one will be best at a particular time. Let's ask your higher self which method of meditation and relaxation will best serve you in a specific instance.

YOGA—Start yoga or get back into it.

MEDITATION IN A SACRED SPACE—Set up a beautiful space and relax your mind.

HOBBIES—Get out your knitting needles, crochet hook, sewing machine, or woodworking tools and get into making something.

WALK IN NATURE—Enjoy fresh air, grounding, natural surroundings, and relaxation.

READ A BOOK—Sit down with a favorite book.

LISTEN TO MUSIC—Put up your feet and turn on your favorite tunes.

TAKE A BATH—Set the mood, light some candles, and relax in water.

WATCH A MOVIE—Grab some popcorn and sit down to watch your favorite movie or try a new one (perhaps nonviolent!).

GARDEN—Tend to your garden, get your hands dirty, and listen to the birds sing.

COOK—Bake or cook to your heart's content and really relish the process of creating something yummy.

SHOP—They do say that shopping is therapy!

EXERCISE—Get outside and move your body or pop on your favorite dance music indoors and move to the beat.

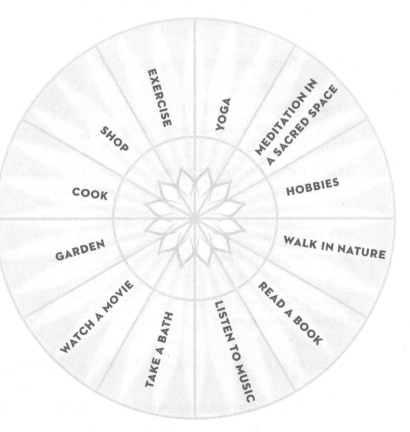

LIFE IMPROVEMENTS

We tend to busy our lives with so much—work, social commitments, family, friends, and so on—that we tend to override what we need to focus on and not listen to what our intuition is telling us. We may need to improve our health, relationships, and more, so let's see where we need to improve.

EAT A BETTER DIET—Your body may be craving healthy, nourishing food right now.

EXERCISE MORE—Get outside and move your body. Do this regularly to get those happy endorphins flowing and to improve your health.

SPEND MORE TIME WITH YOUR PARTNER—Perhaps you need to spend more time with your partner or in the company of those you love.

GET OUTDOORS—Nothing beats Mother Nature.

BE KINDER TO YOURSELF AND OTHERS—Work from the heart and give gratitude always.

INDULGE YOURSELF—Get a massage, a new haircut—anything!!

LEARN NEW SKILLS—Get to that workshop that you have wanted to attend.

TAKE A BREAK—Spend time by yourself—stay home or go on a vacation.

CHANGE YOUR OUTLOOK ON THINGS—Look at life with different eyes and see things in a more positive note.

DISCOVER DIFFERENT PLACES—Change your route

to work—you'll never know what you might find if you change your path.

DECREASE SOCIAL MEDIA USAGE—Ban the use of social media for a few days and see the amazing change it has on your life.

DIVINATION METHODS

Choosing among all the different divination tools you can use can get a little overwhelming. Some days you might have no idea which tool to use. So, let the pendulum choose the best one for you.

PENDULUM—Well this one has a book about it!

ORACLE CARDS—Ask a question and either pull a few cards intuitively or allow some to fly out the deck.

TAROT CARDS—Again, ask a question and intuitively pull cards, let them fly out the deck, or create a card spread.

RUNES—Cast the stones or small pieces of wood with different symbols on them.

MEDITATION—Sit quietly in meditation and allow guidance from above to come in.

TEA LEAVES—Read the tea leaf pattern at the bottom of a cup.

RANDOM PAGE IN A BOOK—I love to intuitively select a book and choose a page. Every time I do this the messages and guidance from the words on the page are spot on.

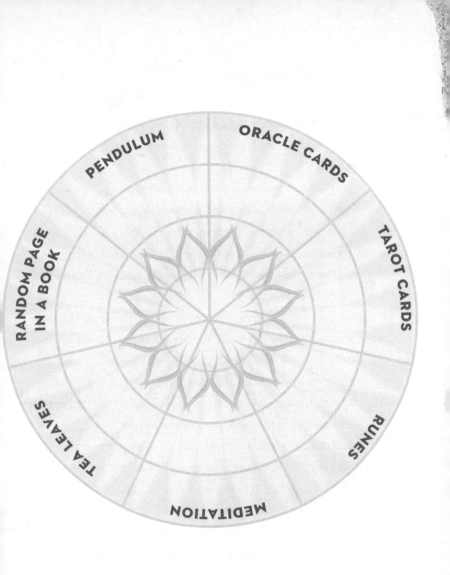

PENDULUM

ORACLE CARDS

TAROT CARDS

RANDOM PAGE IN A BOOK

RUNES

TEA LEAVES

MEDITATION

ALPHABET CIRCLE

You can use this circle to spell out the letters in a worded answer to a question or perhaps to ask the name of your higher self. I received the name of my higher self by using the pendulum with the alphabet circle: Lezley.

Always protect yourself with any of the cleansing methods mentioned previously, such as burning a smudge stick, white light, and so on. I like to burn some of my homemade energy-cleansing incense (dried rosemary, rose petals, white sage, and lavender) when doing this and protect myself with a ring of white light, asking only for my wisdom beyond to join me.

Do not have any fear, as using the pendulum in a circle of letters is not like using a Ouija board. You are always connected to your higher self; however, it's always a good idea to cleanse the space you are working in before proceeding with any spiritual work. I have felt safe using the alphabet circle and only contacted my higher self (Lezley) when asking for words to my questions.

Using this circle takes a bit of practice, as the wedges are quite close together. Be patient and don't rush the answers, as the pendulum may take a while to swing to a letter. You may find it easier to enlarge this circle on another sheet of paper.

I also find that before I receive the first letter, the pendulum likes to rotate around in the center for some time. I think that this is the pendulum and my higher self "getting to know" the circle and where the letters are.

Have fun and enjoy the process, as this is a different spin on the usual pendulum circles.

BLANK CIRCLE #1

Use this blank circle to make your own theme and answers for a pendulum circle.

BLANK CIRCLE #2

Use this blank circle to make your own theme and answers for a pendulum circle.

BLANK CIRCLE #3

Use this blank circle to make your own theme and answers for a pendulum circle.

BLANK CIRCLE #4

Use this blank circle to make your own theme and answers for a pendulum circle.

BLANK CIRCLE #5

Use this blank circle to make your own theme and answers for a pendulum circle.

CONCLUSION

Pendulums are a great tool to use to venture into the realm of divination. Divination is a soulful practice that requires you to go within and seek the guidance you need. Once you start listening to your intuition, tuning into your psychic powers within, you start to see that life has different viewpoints—ones that you never knew existed. You may start to look at everything around you with new eyes—appreciate all the glory and the small things that are right in front of you. Your life may take new directions that differ from the paths you thought were right. Using the pendulum daily in your life can help you attune yourself to your intuition; it can give you that nudge in the right direction or simply answer questions based on your intuitive feelings. It is sometimes difficult to trust the intuitive feelings that we get—the constant feeling that something needs to change and you know what needs to change but you're too fearful of where that change will take you. The pendulum will be your lifelong friend—something you can go to for reassurance, for that second opinion, to open yourself to the spiritual realm, connect to higher beings, and move your life in the right direction.

Time, patience, persistence and trust are all important aspects when using the pendulum. Do not let these discourage you. Great rewards await those who learn to do the work right, so move slowly and lovingly with your new divination tool and watch how your life can unfold in ways you never thought possible. Allow yourself time to use the pendulum; this is a wonderful ritual for your spiritual practice and it's one to treasure and enjoy. The more time you put into your own spiritual practice, be it with the pendulum or not, the more you're going to notice changes in your thoughts, your actions, and your priorities. Trust me, it's for the better! Try to find a quiet place every day—even if it's to swing the pendulum in front of you or simply hold it— just to form a bond and allow your energy and the pendulum's energy to intertwine.

Your pendulum practice is going to be different from everyone else's. There's no right or wrong way to use a pendulum, and what you've learned here is an overview of basic techniques to use. However, throughout your pendulum journey you will notice that your practice may change, evolve, improve, and strengthen as you start finding your unique way of using your pendulum. Always listen to your heart, and if a technique that you see other people doing doesn't quite align with you, don't do it. I am constantly learning new ways to use a pendulum from other people; not all align with how I work, but I appreciate discovering the different ways others use their pendulums. In my journey I have found that when I try to use my pendulum in ways that don't sit quite right with me, this is when I find it very hard to use my pendulum. So remember that just because you have read something or watched someone use a pendulum in a different way from yours, it's not necessarily the right way for you! If you are a beginner in your pendulum work, it can be quite overwhelming to watch experts use a pendulum, and you then believe that what you saw is what you need to do. Not the case at all! Listen to your heart, listen to your body, and work your pendulum to a way that suits you.

So let's get our pendulums out and create a magical alliance with them. Your intuition and higher self will relish the connection that you are making. Choose a pendulum that has sparked something in you, embrace its beauty, hold it lovingly, and allow the magic of subtle energy to give you guidance and direction in life. The connection that you make with your higher self will only get better as time goes by, so enjoy this process. Your life may change dramatically—or not—but it will change for the better and always with love. My life changed for the better, and I look back even just a few years and am forever grateful to be in contact with my "wisdom beyond'" and my divination tools, especially my pendulums! Take what you want from this book and use your pendulums to suit you. Enjoy your journey and, if you feel so inclined, spread the love of pendulums to others!

ABOUT THE AUTHOR

I am married and the mother of two girls. I live in a beautiful cottage surrounded by trees and flowers in suburban Perth, Western Australia.

I run a small online business called Amongst The Wildflowers (www.amongstthewildflowers.com.au) where I sell a wide variety of products ranging from items that I make, to clothing and accessories and spiritual products. A variety of pendulums that I make are available in my shop. I am also a Reiki practitioner, crystal healer, and facilitator of women's circles under the new moon and full moon.

I consider myself quite the creative free spirit. I have many projects in the works and always enjoy learning how to make new creations.

I am also a green witch. I love to work with natural elements and gifts from nature to create magic in my life. I create natural products from homemade tinctures, oils, and essences, and turn them into plant-based remedies and medicine. I am an avid book lover and would prefer to buy books than clothes.

ENDNOTES

Introduction

"The use of dowsing tools": American Society of Dowsers. Accessed September 26, 2018. https://dowsers.org/dowsing-information-and-artifacts/.

"The use of dowsing tools": Nielson, Greg and Polanksy, Joseph. *Pendulum Power*. Destiny Books, 1987.

"The Chinese Emperor Yu has": Geopathology.com. Accessed September 26, 2018. http://geopathology.com/dowsing.html.

"In the mid 1600's, these": Pendulums. Accessed September 26, 2018. https://en.wikipedia.org/wiki/pendulum.

"Pendulum use was then forbidden": Conway, D. J. *A Little Book of Pendulum Magic*. Crossing Press, 2001.

"In 1833, Michel Eugène Chevreul": Michel Eugène Chevreul. Accessed September 26, 2018. https://wikipedia.org/wiki/Michel_Eugene_Chevreul.

"Abbé Mermet invented the 'Mermet,": Energy Devices and Pendulums. Accessed September 26, 2018. www.emeraldinnovations.co.uk.

"The reason it's so difficult": Ideomotor Phenomenon. Accessed September 26, 2018. https://en.wikipedia.org/wiki/Ideomotor_phenomenon.

"During the Vietnam War the": Vibrational Health. Accessed September 26, 2018. www.vibrationalhealth.com.au.

"During the Vietnam War the": Radiesthesia. Accessed September 26, 2018. www.radiesthesia.com.au.

"During the Cold War in": History of Pendulum Dowsing. Accessed September 26, 2018. www.pendulums.com.

INDEX